1001
Motivational Messages and Quotes

Teaching Character Through Sport

Bruce Eamon Brown

ISBN: 1-58518-377-6
Library of Congress Catalog Card Number: 00-108303
Cover Design: Kerry Hartjen
Front cover photos: (Row 1) Al Bello/Getty Images, Scott Barbour/AUS/Allsport; (Row 2) Donald Miralle/Getty Images, Al Bello/Getty Images; (Row 3) Brian Bahr/Allsport, Vincent Laforet/Allsport, Elsa/Allsport
Book layout: Paul Lewis

BK
$15.00

Coaches Choice
P.O. Box 1828
Monterey, CA 93942
www.coacheschoice.com

Dedication

To the two great teams of my life: My family and 32 years of exceptional young people.

Preface

The power of messages often comes in a few well-chosen words. Words initiate thoughts. Thoughts provide motivation. Motivation produces action. A few words can speak volumes. Words coming from the right person at the right moment, can go directly to the heart. One of the greatest leaders in history, Chief Joseph of the Nez Perce instructs us: *"Good words do not last long unless they amount to something......it doesn't require many words to seek the truth."*

The quotes in this book represent a collection and culmination of 30 years of attempting to teach young athletes the lessons of life through sport. I hope that these quotes help improve your life and the lives of the young people you reach.

Being an athlete is an honor that lasts a lifetime, and being a coach is the greatest job in the world.

— Bruce Eamon Brown

Contents

Part I: Coaching and Leadership

To me the coaching profession is one of the noblest and most far-reaching in building manhood. No man is too good to be the athletic coach for youth."
— Amos Alonzo Stagg

"The greatest use of life is to live your life that the use of your life will outlive your life."
— Mack Douglas

No person will completely understand the relationships and emotions involved in coaching until they become a coach. The opportunity to work with highly motivated coaches and athletes in an atmosphere of mutual respect, trust and dependence is unique and priceless. The energy and lifeblood of the team runs through the coach.

The primary role of the coach is to build lifetime character traits in the young people who are in their care. Established standards for effort, behavior and character must be continually taught and corrected by coaches. By helping young men and women understand the difference between right and wrong behavior and to have the courage to live by those standards, the need to bear down and achieve a goal, to recover from mistakes, to put the team ahead of themselves, to accept correction and discipline, to put their heart in their work, and develop a true confidence, coaching becomes an expression of love.

Everyday in the life of a coach provides a chance to change a life.

COACHING CHANGES LIVES

Good coaches plan – *Great coaches* plan every detail, based on a strong personal philosophy.

Good coaches encourage and motivate – *Great coaches* motivate through love and get every ounce of attention and energy from their athletes.

Good coaches understand the game – *Great coaches* understand the game and their athletes and how to teach both.

Good coaches have strong beliefs – *Great coaches* are believed.

Good coaches are positive – *Great coaches* have a positive passion.

Good coaches talk about their expectations – *Great coaches* have athletes who meet their expectations, because they confront incorrect behavior and half efforts and earn the love and respect of the athletes.

Great coaches understand that making coaching a ministry gives more urgency to every minute we spend with young people, and purpose to the strategies we employ. Viewing coaching as an opportunity to hold athletes to the highest standards possible gives eternal value to their lives.

"Coach each boy as if he were your own son."

— Eddie Robinson

"I've come to a frightening conclusion that I am the decisive element in the classroom. It's my personal approach that creates the climate. It's my daily mood that makes the weather. As a teacher, I possess a tremendous power to make a child's life miserable or joyous. I can be a tool of torture or an instrument of inspiration. I can humiliate or humor, hurt or heal. In all situations, it is my response that decides whether a crisis will be escalated or de-escalated and a child humanized or de-humanized."

— Haimginott

"The lesson you teach today is not confined to the walls of your classroom. Once it is implanted in the heart and mind of a child, it can change the world."

— Unknown

"Discipline of others isn't punishment. You discipline to help, to improve, to correct, to prevent, not to punish, humiliate, or retaliate."

— John Wooden

"A great vision is needed, and the man who has it must follow it as the eagle seeks the deepest blue of the sky.

— Crazy Horse/ Tashunkewitko

"Most battles are won before they are fought."

— Sun Tzu – 450 B.C.

"Apart from an innate grasp of tactical concepts, a great coach must possess the essential attributes of leadership which mold men into a cohesive, fighting team with an invincible will to victory."

— General Douglas MacArthur

"Good guys are a dime a dozen, but an aggressive leader is priceless."

— Red Blaik

"Try to set standards that will make other people wish they were on your team."

— Ken Horne

"Don't talk too much or too soon."

— Bear Bryant

"Finish last in coaching, and watch what happens. You know what they call the guy who finished last in medical school? They call him doctor."

— Abe Lemons

"Leadership must be demonstrated, not announced."

— Fran Tarkenton

"You must BE the change that you wish to see in the world."

— Ghandi

"Make sure that team members know they are working with you, not for you."

— John Wooden

"Leadership, like coaching, is fighting for the hearts and souls of men and getting them to believe in you."

— Eddie Robinson

"Our children are like jewels, to be polished by us and presented to the Lord."

— Unknown

"If you hate your job, don't worry, you won't have it for long."

— George Allen

"I am just a common man who is true to his beliefs."

— John Wooden

"Leaders are like eagles... they don't flock. You'll find them one at a time."

— Knute Rockne

"Organization is a habit."

— George Allen

"A real executive goes around with a worried look on his assistants."

— Vince Lombardi

"Coaching is not a natural way of life. Your victories and losses are too clear cut."

— Tommy Prothro

"Timing has a lot to do with the outcome of the rain dance."

— Unknown

"The majority of people pull for the underdog. Heck, even your friends don't like you to be too successful. We've lost enough over the years for me to maintain my friendships."

— Darrell Royal

"Upon the field of friendly strife are sown the seeds that on other fields, on other days, will bear the fruits of victory."

— General Douglas MacArthur

"If you could have won, you should have."

— Chuck Knox

"Single moments, improved or wasted, are the salvation or ruin of all-important interests."

—John Henry, Cardinal Newman

"God judges a leader not by the numbers that are led, but by the numbers that are served."

— Unknown

"Organize, deputize and supervise."

— Biff Jones

"A committee of one, gets things done."

— Joe Ryan

"Train the child in the way he should go, and when he is old he will not turn from it."

— Proverbs 22:6 NIV

"Coaching is a profession of love. You can't coach people unless you love them."

— Eddie Robinson

"Young people need models, not critics."

— John Wooden

"The gem cannot be polished without friction, nor the person perfected without trials."

— Unknown

"I don't talk too much about my battle plan, even after the game is over. I save it for another occasion."

— George Halas

"When you are discussing a successful coach, you are not necessarily drawing a profile of an entirely healthy person."

— Bruce Ogilvie
sports psychologist

"It is what you learn after you know it all that counts."

— John Wooden

"The shortest and surest way to live with honor in the world is to be in reality what we appear to be."

— Socrates

"Wisdom comes from an equal balance of experience and reflection."

— Aristotle

"I am poor and naked, but I am the chief of the nation. We do not want riches, but we want to train our children right."

— Red Cloud
Sioux chief

During the forty-seven game winning streak of the "gentleman coach" Bud Wilkinson, Oklahoma's president, Dr. George L. Cross, was asked to speak about his school's academic goals. His answer: "We are trying to build a university that our football team can be proud of."

"A good scare is often worth more to a man than good advice."

— Ed Howe

"Don Shula is just like Vince Lombardi. You pay the price, but then you get what you pay for."

— Marv Fleming

"The key to success and happiness is to find a middle level. The one problem with football is that there is no middle ground—football is all highs and lows. That brings things out in people that normally wouldn't surface. A lot of good men become Jekylls and Hydes and everyone they touch suffers,"

— Sam Rutigliano

Three Rules of Coaching:

1. Surround yourself with people who can't live without football.

2. Recognize winners. They come in all forms.

3. Have a plan for everything.

— Paul "Bear" Bryant

A True North

Our ships are tossed
Across the night,
Our compass cracked,
For wrong or right.
True North is there,
Or over here?
Confusion rules
Our sea is fear.
Then suddenly a beacon bright
Is shining through
This stormy night.
It's pure and straight
To his true course.
The coach is seen
He is True North.

– Steve Jamison

"Forewarned, forearmed; to be prepared is half the battle."

— Cervantes

"All the education and all the knowledge in the world can't help the poor soul who has no common sense."

— Benjamin Franklin

"Experience is not what happens to a man. It is what a man does with what happens to him."

— Chuck Knox

"It is not the same to talk of the bulls as to be in the bullring."

— Spanish Proverb

"A wise man will make more opportunities than he finds."

— Francis Bacon

"What makes a good coach? Complete dedication."

— George Halas

"I'd rather be a football coach. That way you can lose only 11 games a season. I lost 11 games in December alone."

— Abe Lemons
basketball coach

"A successful coach needs a patient wife, loyal dog, and great quarterback – and not necessarily in that order."

— Bud Grant

"Don't cuss, don't argue with the officials, and don't lose the game."

— John Heisman

"When you are a hammer, everything looks like a nail."

— Anonymous

"The achiever is the only individual who is truly alive. I see no difference in a chair and the man who sits in the chair, unless he is accomplishing something."

— George Allen

"Leaders are chosen to serve; there is always trouble when the leader forgets this."

— Unknown

"One of these days in your travels a man is going to come up to you and show you a nice, brand new deck of cards on which the seal is not yet broken, and this guy is going to offer to bet you that he can make the jack of spades jump out of the deck and squirt cider in your ear. But, son, do not bet this man, for as sure as you stand there, you re going to wind up with an earful of cider."

— Damon Runyon

"If you live long enough, lots of nice things happen."

— George Halas

"Develop a love for details. They usually accompany success."

— John Wooden

"The strongest human instinct is to impart information, the second strongest is to resist it."

— Kenneth Graham

"The wise leader is of service: receptive, yielding, following. The group's members vibration dominates and leads, while the leader follows. But soon, it is the members' consciousness which is transformed. It is the job of the leader to be aware of the group's members process; it is the need of the group member to be received and paid attention to. Both get what they need, if the leader has the wisdom to serve and follow."

— John Heider
The Tao of Leadership

"Motivating through fear may work in the short term to get people to do something, but over the long run I believe personal pride is a much greater motivator. It produces far better results that last for a much longer time."

— John Wooden

"You can't stop at every dog that barks or you'll never get the mail delivered."

— Phog Allen

The Paradoxical Commandments

1. **People are illogical, unreasonable, and self-centered.**
    Love them anyway.

2. **If you do good, people will accuse you of selfish ulterior motives.**
    Do good anyway.

3. **If you are successful, you will win false friends and true enemies.**
    Succeed anyway.

4. **The good you do today will be forgotten tomorrow.**
    Do good anyway.

5. **Honesty and frankness make you vulnerable.**
    Be honest and frank anyway.

6. **The biggest men and women with the biggest ideas can be shot down by the smallest men and women with the smallest minds.**
    Think big anyway.

7. **People favor underdogs but follow only top dogs.**
    Fight for a few underdogs anyway.

8. **What you spend years building may be destroyed overnight.**
    Build anyway.

9. **People really need help but may attack you if you do help them.**
    Help people anyway.

10. **Give the world the best you have and you'll get kicked in the teeth.**
    Give the world the best you have anyway.

— Kent M. Keith

"Basically it all gets down to one thing: players want to play. If they listen, they play."

— John Wooden
(on getting players to listen)

"The strength of the group is the strength of the leaders."

— Vince Lombardi

"Be gentle and you can be bold; be frugal and you can be liberal; avoid putting yourself before others and you can be a leader of men."

— Lao-Tzu

"Don't limit a child to your own learning, for he was born in another time."

— Rabbinical saying

"Leadership can be described in one word – honesty. You must be honest with the players and honest with yourself. Never be afraid to stick up for your players."

— Earl Weaver

"Everybody has a suggestion. Not everybody has a decision. Perhaps that's why there are so few leaders, at least good leaders.

— John Wooden

"Fear of failure can restrict a player; it can kill him as an individual. If one continually worries about failing, he'll get so tight that he will fail. We want to be properly prepared for anything in a game, but we don't want to worry about losing the game. If we lose it… we'll find out why. But one of the reasons shouldn't be that we were so tight that we were afraid at the outset."

— Chuck Noll

"The secret to winning is constant, consistent management."

— Tom Landry

"Make the present good, and the past will take care of itself."

— Knute Rockne

"The next best thing to playing football is coaching it – passing on to kids bursting out of their skins with health and vigor and to teach some of the things you picked up about the game as you went along."

— Red Grange

"People let you wander around in mediocrity as long as you want, but at the top of the hill, enemies await."

— Sam Wyche

"He knew a little about basketball, and he did a good job and then lived happily ever after, and loved his players and received loyalty in return."

— Dean Smith
(on how he hoped to be
remembered as a coach)

"You must have respect, which is part of love, for those under your supervision. Then they will do what you ask and more."

— John Wooden

"Example teaches better than precept. It is the best modeler of the character of men and women. To set a lofty example is the richest bequest a man can leave behind him."

— S. Smiles, American writer

"Know your enemy and know yourself and you can fight a hundred battles without disaster."

— Sun Tzu

"Overcoaching is the worst thing you can do to a player."

— Dean Smith

"I am sure that if a coach has a strong philosophy of life, he will be successful. To sit by and worry about criticism, which too often comes from the misinformed or from those incapable of passing judgement on an individual or a problem, is a waste of time."

— Adolph Rupp

"Adversity can be a great motivator. Football, as anything else, is always a series of problems. Your success will depend on how well you are prepared and how well you handle those problems as they come along."

— Bill Walsh

"Coaching is like taking eagles and teaching them to fly in formation."

— D. Wayne Calloway

"Leadership is a matter of having people look at you and gain confidence by seeing how you react. If you are in control, they are in control."

— Tom Landry

"The speed of the leader determines the rate of the pack."

— Unknown

"I learn teaching from teachers. I learn golf from golfers. I learn winning from coaches."

— Harvey Penick

"It is a very bad thing to become accustomed to good luck."

— Publilius Syrus

"Make a tree good and its fruit will be good, or make a tree bad and its fruit will be bad, for a tree is recognized by its fruit."

— Matthew 12:33 NIV

"If you are going to be a champion, you must be willing to pay a greater price than your opponent."

— Bud Wilkinson

"Regard your soldiers as children, and they may follow you wherever you may lead. Look upon them as your beloved sons and they will stand by you unto death."

— Sun-Tzu

"In a crisis, don't hide behind anything or anybody. They are going to find you anyway."

— Bear Bryant

"Any time you give a man something he doesn't earn, you cheapen him. Our kids earn what they get, and that includes respect."

— Woody Hayes

"In any competitive situation, a chief duty of leadership is to minimize the impact of unexpected conditions and distractions on the team in combat."

— Pat Riley

"You can motivate by fear, and you can motivate by reward. But both those methods are only temporary. The only lasting thing is self-motivation."

— Homer Rice

"The eight laws of learning are explanation, demonstration, imitation, repetition, repetition, repetition, repetition, and repetition."

— John Wooden

"When you get to where you are going, the first thing to do is take care of the horse that got you there."

— Unknown

"Put your information across slowly and repeat it over and over again! Take a difficult point and make it so simple that it will become clear to even the dullard."

— Knute Rockne

"Good coaching is based purely in leadership.... a positive example.... and instilling respect in your players."

— John Wooden

"Success is about having, excellence is about being. Success is about having money and fame, but excellence is being the best you can be."

— Mike Ditka

"There is no such thing as small flaws."

— Don Shula

"No matter how successful he is, every coach eventually reaches a point where a lot of people want somebody else."

— Father's advice
to Bud Wilkinson

"You don't beat people with surprises, you beat them with execution."

— John McKay

"Anybody who gets away with something will come back to get away with a little bit more."

— Harold Schoenberg

"My responsibility is leadership, and the minute I get negative, that is going to have a influence on my team."

— Don Shula

"Our chief want in life is somebody who shall make us do what we can."

— Emerson

"No coach who is sure of himself and his team constantly bawls out his players."

— Jock Sutherland

"The coaches' most powerful tool is love."

— John Wooden

"Either love your players or get out of coaching."

— Bobby Dodd

"Where you cannot drive, you can always look to persuade. A gentle word, a kind look, a good natured smile can work wonders and accomplish miracles. There is a secret pride in every human that revolts at tyranny. You may order and drive an individual, but you cannot make him respect you."

— William Hazlitt

"It is easy to make a mountain out of a molehill. All you do is add dirt."

— Unknown

"The fewer rules a coach has, the fewer rules there are for players to break."

— John Madden

"Kids don't learn leadership from a class – you learn leadership and organization in games."

— John Madden

"Coaches have to watch for what they don't want to see and listen for what they don't want to hear."

— John Madden

"Insanity is doing the same thing over and over and expecting a different result."

— Albert Einstein

"There are no office hours for champions."

— Paul Dietzel

"It is bad coaching to blame your boys for losing a game, even if it is true."

— Jake Gaither

"In handling men, there are three feelings that a man must not possess—fear, dislike and contempt. If he is afraid of men he cannot handle them. Neither can he influence them in his favor if he dislikes or scorns them. He must neither cringe nor sneer. He must have both self-respect and respect for others."

— Herbert Casson,
American writer

"You can motivate players better with kind words than you can with a whip."

—Bud Wilkinson

"Knowledge alone is not enough to get desired results. You must have the more elusive ability to teach and to motivate. This defines a leader; if you can't teach and you can't motivate, you can't lead."

— John Wooden

"If you want to be successful, you have to do what everybody else does and do it better – or you have to do it differently."

— Steve Spurrier

"It ain't what you eat, but how you chew it."

— Delbert McClinton

"Leadership is the ability to lift and inspire."

— Paul Dietzel

"People are in greater need of our praise when they try and fail, than when they try and succeed."

— Unknown

"If you treat an individual as he is, he will remain as he is. But if you treat him as if he were what he ought to be and could be, he will become what he ought to be and could be."

— Goethe

"Four things cannot come back: the spoken word, the spent arrow, the past life, and a neglected opportunity."

— Arabian Proverb

"Players don't care how much I know until they know how much I care."

— Frosty Westering

"Motivation is simple. Eliminate those who aren't motivated."

— Lou Holtz

"I want things to go right all the time, every day."

— Pete Carril

"Gentleman, you are about to play football for Yale. Never again in your life will you do anything so important."

— Tad Jones

Dean Smith on the Dean E. Smith Student Activities Center—

"You've got to wonder about the priorities of a society that allows a basketball coach to work in a place like that."

"You need the qualities of industriousness and enthusiasm within yourself. And if you are a leader, you will soon instill those qualities in those under your supervision by your example."

— John Wooden

"There is a need of staggering magnitude for doing something in our educational program to help children and youth acquire realistic attitudes of self-acceptance.

— Dr. Arthur T. Jersild
In Search of Self

"It is better to build strong children than to try to repair adults."

— Unknown

"If you flatter me, I may not believe you.
If you ignore me, I won't remember you
If you criticize me, I may not like you.
If you encourage me, I won't forget you."

— Chuck Updike

"No written word
Nor spoken plea
Can teach our youths
What they should be.

Nor all the books
On all the shelves.
It's what the teachers
Are themselves."

— Unknown

Part II:
Themes for Teaching Life Skills Through Sport

A COACHES GUIDE

The profession of coaching is an awesome privilege and responsibility. A quality athletic experience should make a significant contribution to the lives of the individual participants. In our present day society, athletics, church and family are some of the few areas where young people are taught life skills and character traits. For those athletes without the benefit of church or strong family, athletics may be the only hope.

Coaches need to recognize that the same components that make athletics so influential in developing positive personal characteristics can also make them equally effective in development of undesirable behaviors. Sport can provide one of the greatest opportunities in a young person's life to learn to be unethical, take short cuts, make excuses, be dishonest, disrespectful, and to cheat. It also may be the greatest place to learn and practice being ethical, honest, humble, fair, courageous, positive, supportive, hard working, coachable, self disciplined, unselfish, persistent, mentally tough, to live with integrity, and to be gracious in both victory and defeat. Which set of behaviors is going to be learned and demonstrated in the sporting arena is the sole responsibility and obligation of the coach. The coach must be able to teach, correct and model ethical behaviors and positive character traits.

DON'T LEAVE IT TO CHANCE

Sports are given credit for teaching life skills. Does this automatically happen by being close to, or in the action? Although it may be true for some athletes, coaches cannot make the assumption that simply being part of an athletic experience will ensure that the participants will learn these lessons. Like anything else we hope to accomplish in our sport, <u>we must plan for it, and teach it if we want it to happen.</u>

One of the best methods for coaches to ensure these essential life lessons are learned is to identify what your particular sport is capable of teaching the participants and then to take the time to focus on each one as a *theme of the day or week.* We have used this model of teaching and correcting positive lessons in every sport we have coached. It will require some time and planning by your coaching staff to prepare for these presentations, just as you do for any other part of your practice.

PLANNING

Before the season begins, one of the tasks of the coaching staff should be to identify which lessons they want to focus on during the year and then schedule them into the practice calendar. Each day, you should plan a few minutes into the beginning and/or end of every practice to have a presentation that emphasizes the theme for the week. It will require some research and thought to make it meaningful to your team.

After you have decided on the themes for the season, it may benefit you to fit them on to your game calendar. Although your main focus should be on your own   athletes, some themes may be more appropriately scheduled based on your opponent. For example, in a week you are going to play a team that has a history of unsportsmanlike behavior, you may choose to have the theme be poise. Keeping your focus on your preparation and demonstrating poise so your opponent's choices do not draw your players into poor behavior or penalties.

One coach can take the responsibility for the themes, in order to schedule presenters, do bulletin boards, player letters, etc., but all coaches need to participate in the presenting, teaching, correcting and modeling of the themes.

PRESENTERS
Presenters have proven to be more effective when they are allowed to volunteer and also to choose which theme they want to present. We have used a variety of presenters with equal success.

<u>Coaches</u>: Coaches need to be part of every presentation. Whether it is introducing the speaker or the theme, following up with reminders during or at the end of practice, or making the presentation, they are an essential ingredient. Often times, coaches will conclude practice with a reminder and a chance for athletes to talk briefly on what they have learned about the theme and how it applies to the sport or their life outside sport. When you are beginning, it may be easier to do these follow-ups in   smaller groups, especially if it is a larger team activity (e.g., track, football, etc.). The head coach needs to continue to pull the themes together throughout the season.

<u>Athletes</u>: Once you have established themes as a tradition in your program, athletes will quickly volunteer for an opportunity to present (sometimes a year ahead of time). But when you are just beginning this program, they may be reluctant. Encourage your team leaders to take a theme and allow them to go over it with you before they present. Always allow your athletes to respond to the presentation with thoughts of their own or questions. There have been times when we have asked specific athletes to present certain themes in order to help them make behavioral changes. An athlete who may struggle with sportsmanship or poise can greatly benefit from preparing and addressing a relevant topic in front of his team and coaches.

<u>Staff:</u> Having an administrator, faculty and staff member present once during the week is a great way to build a relationship between your team and the school. It also gives them some insight and appreciation for what you are trying to do for the athlete's lives outside of the sport and the focus on winning games. You will be surprised how flattered people are to be asked by an athlete or coach to address the team. We have had some years where

we asked athletes to nominate the teachers to us who they would like to have speak. Players and coaches are always encouraged to ask questions or make comments from their perspective that will assist in the understanding of the theme. After a staff member has made this connection with the team, we often see an improved relationship between the staff member and the student/athlete and, subsequently, an increased attendance at games.

Community Members: We have had tremendous success with having members of the community present. There is usually a wealth of talent in your community from which to draw. Pastors, ex-athletes, people who have overcome adversity, community leaders, parents, have all been effective presenters. One of the things we have done to form a historical connection with the program is to have former athletes come back and present to the current players. Having former athletes come back and speak has become a tradition. Establishing any kind of positive tradition always gives additional value to an individual's athletic experience, and an historical perspective to an athletic program. This has been particularly effective before a "big game" or playoff.

SPOTLIGHTING – PUBLIC ACKNOWLEDGEMENT
Once a theme has been presented, "spotlighting" is one method we use to acknowledge positive behavior or behavioral changes in our team members. It is done by simply having one person (coach or athlete) "spotlight" another person by making a brief, positive statement about that individual which incorporates the theme. Then the person spoken about, in turn, "spotlights" another person. "I would like to recognize Mike for the *enthusiasm* he brings to practice everyday. His *enthusiasm* to get better has helped improve our whole team. Mike then identifies another team member for something he has done with *enthusiasm*. "Ron's *enthusiasm* toward conditioning helps me keep working when I don't think I can go any longer." And the "spotlight" continues to be passed around for just a few minutes. This exercise doesn't have to go very long or mention every person in the group, but it does have to be sincere. On teams where there are large numbers of participants, in order to have players become comfortable, we will usually start "spotlighting" with players in smaller groups, with the teammates and coaches they are most often with. The coach has to have a feel for how to encourage sincere participation and know when to conclude the exercise.

- Spotlighting is a great opportunity to publicly acknowledge positive behavior and changes that have occurred.

- Acknowledgment of improvement is one of the most powerful methods of reinforcing the life lessons we are attempting to teach.

- Identifying behaviors that are connected to the sport gives the activity more credibility.

- Once any theme has been introduced to the team, the coach and players should keep coming back to it as positive behaviors and choices are witnessed.

- Catching young people doing things well is far more important than catching them doing things wrong.

- Any kind of acknowledgement whether public or private shows value for the athlete and the lesson.

- When it comes to teaching character traits, small acknowledgements tend to lead to bigger accomplishments.

GAME DAY

During pre-game, we give our athletes a quick reminder of the theme and how it and others can be applied during competition. At our post-game meetings, we normally have a full-team spotlight session that again focuses on the theme. Athletes and coaches spotlight based on what they learned about the theme and how they used it both in and out of athletics.

We have had many years when the athletes were comfortable enough to have the post-game spotlight session to be open to family and friends of the team. It is up to the coach to extend an invitation to the family and friends to come into the team-meeting room and listen. This step has been an extremely positive experience and also one that allows the people outside of the team to see values that are being taught and to gain insight into how players and coaches relate, experience the emotion of preparation, and are affected by the performance of the participants.

I often have parents thank me for the opportunity to gain insight into the inner workings of the team. They are pleasantly surprised to hear their own son or daughter speak or be spoken about in terms of valuable life skills learned from a game. They are thankful that the lessons and ethics that they have been trying to instill in their own children are being identified, taught, corrected and encouraged by coaches and teammates.

Because of the emotion of the game or the feelings that occurred during the preparation period leading up to the game, the week to prepare, some of the most important, long-lasting lessons learned often come out during post-game spotlighting with a room filled with teammates, family and friends. For example, some of the comments made at the conclusion of the week where the theme was "courage" were:

- A player who had just been recognized for making a big play in a game, passed on the spotlight by saying: "I would like to spotlight...... who is playing football for the first time. I am proud of him for the courage he had to try out for the football team. It takes a lot more courage to attempt something you've never tried before than it does for an experienced player to make a big play."

- "I would like to recognize........,; sometimes, a simple thing like raising your hand and asking questions in math class takes more courage than playing football."

- "........ showed real courage last weekend by walking away from a situation that was potentially going to get him in trouble and maybe make him ineligible."

- "......... was faced this week with a difficult personal decision, and I watched as he took a stand against something that he knew was wrong, and his courage to stand up for what he knew was right made it easier for the rest of us to also have the courage to make the same decision."

Athletics can be a life-changing experience for the athletes. Their strong desire to play and to please their coaches and teammates provides some of the best chances to teach lessons that will last a lot longer than any physical skill or undefeated season.

The following themes are supported by famous, meaningful quotes. We use these inspirational messages for bulletin boards, signs on players' lockers, letters to players and parents, and presentations.

Enthusiasm

"The successful man has enthusiasm. Good work is never done in cold blood; heat is needed to forge anything. Every great achievement is the story of a flaming heart."
— Harry Truman

As a theme of the week, enthusiasm is always fun. It rewards people for enjoying what they are doing. Enthusiasm is powerful: it produces better, more eager workers, who in turn will produce a better product. What a great gift for people at a young age to be able to learn to put their hearts in their work and let it show. Coach Wooden uses enthusiasm as one of the cornerstones of his Pyramid of Success. Enthusiasm is truly contagious, and having teammates identify it in each other can be the quickest method of spreading the fire. Coaches need to bring their own love for the game for the athletes and for teaching with them everyday. Coaches should teach and model how to love the game as well as play it.

It is always easy to find guest presenters who have enthusiasm. Bring them in and let the fun begin.

"If a man loves the labour of his trade, apart from any question of success or fame, the gods have called him."

— Robert Louis Stevenson

"ENTHUSIASM is the fire in our furnace, it is the spark that keeps us going in high gear. It makes going great.

Enthusiasm brings on Excitement
Excitement then produces Energy
Energy generates Extra Effort
Extra Effort develops Excellence"

— Frosty Westering

"Dreams are wiser than waking."

— Black Elk
Uglala Sioux

"Most powerful is he that is his own power."

— Seneca

"Don't go to the grave with life unused."

— Bobby Bowden

"To be *average* is to be forgotten once you pass from this life. The successful are remembered for their contributions, the failures are remembered because they tried. The *average,* the silent majority, are just forgotten."

— Anonymous

"I like the dreams of the future better than the history of the past."

— Thomas Jefferson

"Merit begets confidence; confidence begets enthusiasm; enthusiasm conquers the world."

— Walter Cottingham

"Everyone should carefully observe which way his heart draws him, and then choose that way with all his strength."

— Hasidic saying

"My hobby is my work. I love it so much, it is not work."

— Dick Vermeil

"Things turn out best for those who make the best of the way things turn out."

— Art Linkletter

"Success is not the result of spontaneous combustion. You must set yourself on fire."

— Reggie Leach

"People who feel good about themselves produce good results."

— Spencer Johnson, M.D. & Kenneth Blanchard, Ph.D.
The One Minute Manager

"I hope that I may always desire more than I can accomplish."

— Michelangelo

"Worry is a futile thing, it's somewhat like a rocking chair, although it keeps you occupied, it doesn't get you anywhere."

— Anonymous

"For the raindrop, joy is entering the river."

— Ghalib

"If you are bored with life, if you don't get up every morning with a burning desire to do things – you don't have enough goals."

— Lou Holtz

"A man is not old until regrets take the place of dreams."

— John Barrymore

"If you can't get enthusiastic about your work, it's time to get alarmed – something is wrong. Compete with yourself. Set your teeth and dive into the job of breaking your own record. No one keeps his enthusiasm automatically. Enthusiasm must be nourished with new actions, new aspirations, new efforts, new vision. It is one's own fault if his enthusiasm is gone; he has failed to feed it. If you want to turn hours into minutes, renew your enthusiasm."

— Papyrus Old Egyptian Historical Papers

"You only live once, but if you do it right, once is enough."

— Joe E. Lewis

"It is impossible to excel at something you don't enjoy."

— Jack Nicklaus

"The greatest evil that can befall a man is that he should come to think evil of himself."

— Goethe

"Make each day your masterpiece. You have control over that."

— John Wooden

"The world belongs to positive, energetic people."

— Jon Frazier

"It's a funny thing about life---if you refuse to accept anything but the best, you often get it."

— Somerset Maugham

"Let your light shine...."

— Matthew 5:16

"I may not be the lion, but it was left up to me to give the lion's roar."

— Winston Churchill

"Most people die before they are fully born. Creativeness means to be born before you die."

— Eric Fromm

"I like people at their prime enthusiasm, when they're riding a crest. Promote a guy and he'll be dying to do good work for you."

— Clint Eastwood

"There is not much to do but to bury a man when the last of his dreams are dead."

— W.M. Carmuth

"Every man is enthusiastic at times. One man has enthusiasm for 30 minutes, another for 30 days, but it is the man who has it for 30 years who makes a success of his life."

— Edward Butler
American scientist

"None are so old as those who have outlived enthusiasm."

— Thoreau

"Life is too short to be little."

— Disrali

"I just love the game of basketball so much. The Game! I don't need the 18,000 people screaming and all the peripheral things. To me, the most enjoyable part is the practice and the preparation."

— Bobby Knight

"Be a tough-minded optimist."

— Frosty Westering

"Every time you think you are not happy, say 'I am happy.' Say it strongly to yourself, even if your feelings are contradictory. Remember, it is your self-image and not you. Just as fast as fish can move in the water, you can instantly change to a happy, balanced attitude."

— Tarthang Tulku Rinpoche

"He who stops being better, stops being good."

— Oliver Cromwell

"To play ball was all I lived for. I used to like to play so much that I loved to take infield practice. Hitting – I could do that all day. I couldn't wait to go to the ballpark. I hated it when we got rained out."

— Mickey Mantle

"To love what you do and feel that it matters, how could anything be more fun?"

— **Katherine Graham**

"I definitely accepted the responsibility of being the team leader. The players know what I'm capable of. More important, they know I have a can't fail attitude."

— **Dominique Wilkens**

"I probably have a different mental approach to swimming than most people. I actually enjoy training."

— **Dawn Fraser**

"I was born to be a runner. I simply love to train."

— **Mary Decker**

"I am the greatest builder in the world. I am the foundation of every triumph. No matter what your position is, I can better it. My name is enthusiasm."

— **Anonymous**

"As a man thinketh, so is he; and as a man chooseth, so is he and so is nature."

— **Ralph Waldo Emerson**

"You live up – or down – to your expectations."

— Lou Holtz

"If you aren't fired with enthusiasm, you'll be fired with enthusiasm."

— Vince Lombardi

"The universe is change; our life is what our thoughts make it."

— Marcus Aurelius Antoninus

"If it is to be, it is up to me."

— Frosty Westering

"You are either green and growing, or ripe and rotting."

— Frosty Westering

"It is not different than little kids who go out and play for the fun of it. We're just big kids playing a game. I love playing and enjoy the thrill of the competition."

— Wayne Gretzky

"Imagination is more important than knowledge."

— Albert Einstein

"Enthusiasm is the inspiration of the great."

— **Christian Bovee**

"If you are killing time, it is not murder, it is suicide."

— **Lou Holtz**

"The best is yet to be, so do it well."

— from *The Man Without a Face*

"Every belief is a limit to be examined and transcended."

— **John C. Lilly**

"The poor man is not he who is without a cent, but he who is without a dream."

— **Kemp**

"Every moment of your life, including this one, is a fresh start."

— **Unknown**

"Once the human mind is stretched by a new idea, it never returns to its original size."

— **Oliver Wendell Holmes**

"Whatever one believes to be true either is true or becomes true in one's mind."

— John C. Lilly

"Shared joy is joy doubled. Shared sorrow is sorrow halved."

— Unknown

"It is more probable that your attitude, rather than your aptitude, will determine your altitude in life."

— Unknown

"Everything may be taken from us except the last of the human freedoms—our ability to choose our own attitude in any situation,"

— Victor Frankl

Work Habits

"Before I get in the ring, I'd have already won or lost it on the road. The real part is won or lost somewhere far away from witnesses – behind the lines, in the gym and out there on the road, long before I dance under those lights."

— Muhammad Ali

One of the most important character traits young people can learn from an athletic experience and carry into other classes and eventually their profession, is the ability to work. Good coaches expect and accept only the best efforts from their athletes everyday. Along with the physical part of work habits comes focus, initiative and attention to detail. Working hard does not come naturally. It can be taught by positive, demanding leadership. Work is reinforced by success. It becomes appreciated by teammates. It becomes who you are as an individual and proudly spreads to the entire team family. It is the shared joy and satisfaction of an all-out individual and team effort. Its achievement fosters deep and lasting team friendship, loyalty, respect and love.

Once good work habits are developed, it is essential that all success enjoyed by the individual athlete or the group is attributed back to the preparation that preceded the game. This step becomes part of the teaching model for future teams.

"Industriousness is the most conscientious, assiduous, and inspired type of work. A willingness to, an appetite for, hard work must be present for success. Without it you have nothing to build on."

— John Wooden

"The time will come when winter will ask what you were doing all summer."

— Henry Clay
American Statesman

"If I do not practice one day, I know it. If I do not practice the next day, the orchestra knows it. If I do not practice the third day, the whole world knows it."

— Ignace Paderewski
Polish Pianist

"Remember this your lifetime through,
Tomorrow there will be more to do.
And failure waits for those who stay
With some success made yesterday.
Tomorrow, you must try once more,
And even harder than before."
— Unknown

"Even if you are on the right track, you'll get run over if you just sit there."

— Will Rogers

"What we are born with is God's gift to us. What we do with it is our gift to God."

— **Anonymous**

"You never know how a horse will pull until you hook him to a heavy load."

— **Bear Bryant**

The Six W's: "Work will win when wishing won't."

— **Todd Blackledge**

"When I was young, I never wanted to leave the court until I got things exactly correct. My dream was to become a pro."

— **Larry Bird**

"A decade after an average athlete graduates, everyone will have forgotten when and where he played. But every time he speaks, everyone will know whether he was educated."

— **Rev. Theodore Hesburgh**
University of Notre Dame

"You can't ever work too much because there is no such thing as being in too good condition. You can't ever lift too many weights because you can't ever be too strong. You can't ever wrestle too much, because you can always do better."

— **Dan Gable**

"I am a slow walker, but I never walk back."

— Abraham Lincoln

"The prospect who does what is required of him is a player. When he does more, he becomes an athlete."

— Hank Iba

"The individual who is mistake-free is also probably sitting around doing nothing. And that is a very big mistake."

— John Wooden

"Maybe you can't play over your head at all. Maybe it's just potential you never knew you had."

— Fran Tarkenton

"Being average is to return no interest for God's investment in you."

— Anonymous

"If people knew how hard I have had to work to gain my mastery, it wouldn't seem wonderful at all."

— Michelangelo

"If you sacrifice early, you'll win late."

— Charles Haley

"Grit… is intensity. Grit is the ability to enjoy responding to intimidation and adversity."

> — **Norm Evans**

"The greatest of all faults is to be conscious of none."

> — **Thomas Carlyle**
> English author

"The difference between failure and success is doing a thing nearly right and doing it exactly right."

> — **Edward C. Simmons**
> American painter

"When you see a successful individual, a champion, you can be very sure that you are looking at an individual who pays great attention to the perfection of minor details."

> — **John Wooden**

"Do you not know that your body is a temple of the Holy Spirit, who is in you, whom you have received from God? You are not your own; you were bought at a price. Therefore, honor God with your body."

> — **I Corinthians 6:19-20**

"Whatever your hands find to do, do it with all your might…"

> — **Ecclesiastes 9:10a** NIV

"If my life had been made up of eight-hour work days, I don't believe I could have accomplished a great deal. This country would not amount to as much as it does if the young men of 50 years ago had been afraid that they might earn more than they were paid for."

— Thomas Edison

"The harder you work, the harder it is to surrender."

— Vince Lombardi

"The Lord didn't burden us with work. He blessed us with it."

— Unknown

"One of life's most painful moments comes when we must admit that we didn't do our homework, that we are not prepared."

— Merlin Olsen

"You don't develop good teeth by eating mush."

— Red Blaik

"The only thing wrong with doing nothing is that you never know when you are finished."

— Unknown

"Even when I went to the playground, I never picked the best players. I picked guys with less talent, but who were willing to work hard, who had the desire to be great."

— Earvin "Magic" Johnson

"Pray devoutly, but hammer stoutly."

— William Benham

"I'll work from dawn to exhaustion. If there is not a crisis, I'll create one."

— Lou Holtz

"The only thing that counts is your dedication to the game. You run on your own fuel; it comes from within you."

— Paul Brown

"I can't believe that God put us on this earth to be ordinary."

— Lou Holtz

"At God's footstool to confess,
A poor soul knelt and bowed his head.
'I failed' he cried. The Master said,
'Thou didst thy best, that is success.'"

— Anonymous

"The quality of a person's life is in direct proportion to his commitment to excellence, regardless of his chosen field of endeavor."

— Vince Lombardi

"You can't make a great play unless you do it first in practice."

— Chuck Noll

"To be satisfied with yourself is a sure sign that all forward motion is about to stop."

— Unknown

"I'm a determined person. And if I've got an objective, I'll make hours of sacrifice – whatever efforts are needed. Some people call it plodding. The word is somewhat downgraded, but I'd rather be a plodder and get some place than have charisma and not make it."

— Gerald Ford

"Out of clutter, find simplicity. From discord, find harmony. In the middle of difficulty, lies opportunity."

— Albert Einstein,
(on his rules of work)

"I never blame failures – there are too many complicated situations in life, but I am absolutely merciless toward lack of effort."

— F. Scott Fitzgerald

"I never knew an early-rising, hard working, prudent man, careful of his earnings and strictly honest, who complained of hard luck. A good character, good habits and hard work are impregnable to the assaults of all ill-luck that fools ever dreamed."

— Joseph Addison

"What you get for free, costs too much."

— Jean Anouilh

"Do not confuse activity with achievement."

— John Wooden

"I see no virtue where I smell no sweat."

— Francis Quarles

"You have to motivate yourself through pride. You must push yourself mentally and physically. A lot of people say John Havlicek never gets tired. Well, I get tired, it's just a matter of pushing myself. I say to myself 'He's as tired as I am, who is going to win the mental battle?'"

— John Havlicek

"Spectacular achievements are always preceded by unspectacular preparation."

— Roger Staubach

"Because a thing seems difficult for you, do not think it is impossible for anyone to accomplish. But whatever is possible for another, believe that you too are capable of it.

— Marcus Aurelius Antoninus

"Repeated actions are stored as habits. If the repeated actions aren't fundamentally sound, then what comes out in a game can't be sound. What comes out will be bad habits."

— Chuck Knox

"Action may not always bring happiness; but there is no happiness without action."

— Benjamin Desraeli

"The great thing in the world is not so much where we stand as in what direction we are moving."

— Oliver Wendell Holmes

"My determination more than made up for any lack of speed, height, weight, or whatever else I wasn't supposed to have."

— Jack Lambert

"Learn to do things right and then do them right every time."

— Bob Knight

"A guy who gives you less than what he has to give is, one, telling you what he thinks of you, and two, telling you what he thinks of himself."

— Pete Carill

"Practice without improvement is meaningless."

— Chuck Knox

Courage

*"Being courageous requires no exceptional qualifications, no magic formula,
no special combination of time, place and circumstance.
It is an opportunity that sooner or later is presented to us all."*

— John F. Kennedy

When introducing the *theme of courage* to our athletes, we have found that often we must first change their perception of courage. It is not always something that is a dramatic or newsworthy event. More often, real courage can be seen in small decisions and choices that individual people make on a daily basis. Decisions they make when they are alone and those made in the presence of witnesses both apply. Once real courage has been described in this bigger picture, athletes begin to recognize courage in their own lives and the lives of the people around them. They begin to appreciate the courage it takes to practice hard when no one is watching, to continue trying when you don't immediately succeed, to see the courage required for others who have battles different than your own, and to discipline themselves to stand alone with their personal beliefs at all times.

The "spotlighting" of courage will subsequently spread from athletes and their sport, and will begin to include decisions around school, on weekends and with their family. Athletes come to understand that most people have far more courage than they give themselves credit for in most situations. Once discovered in themselves, acts of courage are easier to repeat. Once seen in others, teammates and family, courageous choices are more appreciated and modeled.

"One man with courage makes a majority."

— Andrew Jackson

"Courage is a birthright."

— Unknown

"Courage is the first of human qualities because it is the quality which guarantees all the others."

— Sir Winston Churchill

"Courage is resistance to fear, mastery of fear – not absence of fear."

— Anonymous

"Ingenuity, plus courage, plus work, equals miracles."

— Bob Richards

"I believe in the Sun even when it is not shining,
I believe in Love even when I feel it not,
I believe in God even when He is silent."

— words found on a cellar wall
in Cologne after World War II

"Courage means being afraid to do something, but still doing it."

— Knute Rockne

"The Lord is my strength, of whom should I be afraid?"

— Psalm 27:1

"Be strong and take heart and wait on the Lord."

— Genesis 28:15 NIV

"The wicked flee when no one is chasing them! But the Godly are bold as lions."

— Proverbs 28:1

"When you cannot make up your mind which of two evenly balanced courses of action you should take – choose the bolder."

— General W.J. Slim

"The test of tolerance comes when we are in a majority; the test of courage comes when we are in a minority."

— Ralph W. Sockman D. D.

"Get some belly."

— Chuck Knox

"The men who succeed best in public life are those who take the risk of standing by their own convictions."

— James Garfield

"Faith dares the soul to go further than we can see."

— **William Clarke**

"Man can not discover new oceans unless he has the courage to lose sight of the shore."

— **Andre Gide**
French novelist

"The greatness of our fear shows us the littleness of our faith."

— **Anonymous**

"Until one is committed, there is hesitancy, the chance to draw back, always inefffectiveness."

— **Goethe**

"Whatever you can do or dream you can, begin it. Boldness has genius, power and magic in it."

— **Goethe**

"To see what is right and not to do it, is lack of courage."

— **Confucius**

"Security is not the absence of danger, it is the presence of God."

— **Unknown**

"Never undertake anything for which you would not have the courage to ask the blessing of heaven."

— Georg Christian Lichtenberg

"The most sublime courage I have ever witnessed has been among that class too poor to know they possessed it, and too humble for the world to discover it."

— George Bernard Shaw

"They that wait upon the Lord shall renew their strength. They shall mount up with wings, like eagles, They shall run and not be weary, they shall walk and not faint."

— Isaiah 40:31

"There's a point to fear. But there's an immobility to it, too. Fear can make you avoid risk and adventure, and hide behind a mask of security. Fear can save our lives, but it can also shrivel us up, make us play things safe and sometimes deny us our greatest joys."

— Donn Moomaw

"'Not by might nor by power, but by my spirit,' says the Lord Almighty."

— Zecharaiah 4:6

"All progress has resulted from people who took unpopular positions."

— Adlai Stevenson

"Life only demands from you the strength that you possess, only one feat is possible, not to have run away."

— Dag Hammarskjold

"Be not afraid of sudden fear."

— Book of Proverbs

"All glory comes from daring to begin."

— Eugene F. Ware

"Want for the Lord and he will come save you! Be brave, stouthearted and courageous."

— Psalm 27:14

"Don't be too timid about your actions. All life is an experiment."

— Ralph Waldo Emerson

"It is better to be hated for what you are than loved for what you are not."

— Andre Gide
French Novelist

"Keep your eyes open for spiritual danger; stand true to the Lord; act like a man; be strong."

— Corinthians 16:13

"To reach out for another is to risk involvement.
To expose one's feelings is to risk exposing your true self.
To place your ideas, your dreams, before a crowd is to risk their loss.
To love is to risk not being loved in return.
To live is to risk dying.
To hope is to risk despair.
To try is to risk failure.
But risks must be taken, because the greatest hazard
in life is to risk nothing.
The person who risks nothing, does nothing,
has nothing, and is nothing.
They may avoid suffering and sorrow, but they cannot learn,
feel, change, grow, love, live.
Chained by their attitudes, they are a slave,
they have forfeited their freedom.
Only a person who risks is free."

— Unknown

"Take pride in yourself. Be your own person. Don't do things because everyone else does them. Don't be part of the crowd. Dare to be different. Never be afraid to stand up for what you believe to be right, even when it means standing alone."

— Jack Lambert

"Three daily reminders: Have courage to say no. Have the courage to face the truth. Have the courage to do the right thing because it is right."

— W. Clement Stone

"We need people who influence their peers and who cannot be detoured from their convictions by peers who do not have the courage to have any convictions."

— Joe Paterno

Integrity

"Choices are the hinges of destiny."

— Unknown

A person of integrity has depth of character, a completeness and soundness of foundation. This depth is shown as honesty, sincerity, reliability, respect, humility, and loyalty. Introducing integrity as a theme is often as simple as identifying the different behavioral components. By having presenters qualify these areas, the athletes can start to look for the traits in everyone around them. For the most part, these traits are an area of life that are clearly distinguishable and identifiable. They are either part of a person or they are not. They can be learned and changed, since all the components are student-owned choices. It doesn't require much time to have athletes discover that integrity is easy to see, and that there is little gray area in actually living these traits. Once integrity has been defined, student/athletes have little difficulty finding examples to spotlight.

Integrity, like courage, involves daily choices, and those choices will speak for themselves in word and deed.

"To believe in something and not live it is dishonest."

— Ghandi

"Character is destiny."

— Heraclitus

"I am not bound to win, but I am bound to be true. I am not bound to succeed, but I am bound to live up to what light I have."

— Abraham Lincoln

"Character is that which reveals moral purpose, exposing the class of things a man chooses or avoids."

— Aristotle

"The true test of character is not how much we know how to do, but how we behave when we don't know what to do."

— John Holt

"Discipline and diligence are up there on the list, but one of the most important qualities of many really successful people is humility. If you have a degree of humility about you, you have the ability to take advice, to be coachable, teachable. A humble person never stops learning."

— Todd Blackledge

"Class never runs scared. It is sure footed and confident in the knowledge that you can meet life head on and handle whatever comes along.

Class never makes excuses. It takes its lumps and learns from past mistakes.

Class is considerate of others. It knows that good manners are nothing more than a series of small sacrifices.

Class can walk with kings and keep its virtue, and talk with crowds and keep the common touch.

Everyone is comfortable with a person who has class—because he is comfortable with himself.

If you have class, you don't need much of anything else.

If you don't have it, no matter what else you have, it doesn't make much difference."

— Unknown

"Picking an assistant coach, the first thing I was interested in was the man's character."

— Woody Hayes

"Try measuring your wealth by what you are, rather than what you have."

— Unknown

"The game of life is a game of boomerangs. Our thoughts, deeds, and words return to us sooner or later with astounding accuracy."

— Florence Scovel Shinn

"The wise and moral man shines like a fire on the hilltop."

— Unknown

"All that we are is the result of what we have thought."

— Buddha

"It is only in our decisions that we are important."

— Jean-Paul Sartre

"The man who cannot believe in himself, cannot believe in anything else. The basis of all integrity and character is whatever faith we have in our own integrity."

— Roy L. Smith
Clergyman

"You can easily judge a man by how he treats a person that can do nothing for him."

— Unknown

"Not always right in all men's eyes, but faithful to the light within."

— Oliver Wendell Holmes

"Fame is a vapor, popularity an accident, riches take wings and only one thing endures – character."

— Horace Greeley

"Class always shows."

— **Paul Brown**

"Character is what you are in the dark."

— **Dwight L. Moody**

"He who floats with the current, who does not guide himself according to higher principles, who has no ideal, no real standards – such a man is a mere article of the world's furniture – a thing to be moved, instead of a living and moving thing – an echo not a voice."

— **Henri Frederic Amiel**
Swiss philosopher

"The measure of a man's real character is what he would do if he would never be found out."

— **Thomas MacCauley**
English writer and statesman

In any moment of decision, the best thing you can do is the right thing. The worst thing you can do is nothing."

— **Theodore Roosevelt**

"I care not what others think of what I do, but I care very much about what I think I do. That is character."

— **Theodore Roosevelt**

"Try not to become a man of success, but rather try to become a man of value."

— **Albert Einstein**

"How hard you work at correcting your faults reveals your character."

— **John Wooden**

"Look for players with character and ability. But remember, character comes first."

— **Joe Gibbs**

"Make the most of yourself, for that is all there is to you."

— **Emerson**

"A good name is seldom regained. When character is gone all is gone, and one of the richest jewels of life is lost forever."

— **J. Hawes**
American clergyman & author

"I do not want merely to possess a faith; I want a faith that possesses me."

— **Charles Kingsley**

"Character cannot be made except by a steady, long-continued process."

— **Phillip Brooks**
Episcopal bishop

"There is a choice you have to make, in everything you do. And you must always keep in mind the choice you make, makes you."

— **Anonymous**

"To win by cheating, by umpire error, or by an unfair stroke of fate is not really to win at all. If athletic competition does not teach this, then what more valuable lesson is there to learn than that we have a responsibility to stand up for what is right?"

— **Pete Dawkins**

"I have always thought the actions of men are the best interpreters of their thoughts."

— **John Locke**

"Be more concerned with your character than your reputation. Character is what you really are. Reputation is just what people say you are."

— **John Wooden**

"I hope I shall always possess firmness and virtue enough to maintain what I consider the most enviable of all titles, the character of an honest man."

— **George Washington**

"Morale and attitude are the fundamentals to success."

— **Bud Wilkinson**

"Somewhere along the line you have to trust someone. You've got to be clever enough to pick someone who's smart and wholesome and worthy – and then just listen to what they say."

— Dave Joyner

"Talent is God-given, be humble; fame is man-given, be thankful; conceit is self-given, be careful."

— Anonymous

"Send the harmony of a great desire vibrating through every fiber of your being. Find a task that will call forth your faith, your courage, your perseverance, and your spirit of sacrifice. Keep your hands and your soul clean, and your conquering current will flow freely."

— Thomas Dreier
American author

"The eternal verities always prevail, you'll never lick them. That is loyalty, honesty, sincerity, discipline and dedication....all the things that are worthwhile. They will always be with us."

— Paul Brown

"Life is a grindstone. Whether it grinds you down or polishes you up depends on what you're made of."

— Jacob M. Braude

"If I were ever prosecuted for my religion, I truly hope there would be enough evidence to convict me."

— John Wooden

"When wealth is lost – nothing is lost.
When health is lost – something is lost.
When character is lost – all is lost."

— Unknown

"Truth has no special time of its own. Its hour is now – always."

— Albert Schweitzer

"The greatest truths are simplest, so likewise the greatest men."

— Unknown

Rationalization: "Allowing my mind to find reason to excuse what my spirit knows is wrong."

— Romans 2:21
Amplified

"For when that One Great Scorer comes, to mark against your name, He writes – not that you won or lost – but how you played the game."

— Grantland Rice

"I have prepared for death all my life by the life I lived."

— Socrates

"Many people are bothered by those passages in the Scripture which they cannot understand; but as for me, I always noticed what the passages in Scripture which trouble me the most are those I do understand."

— Mark Twain

"I pray thee, O God, that I may be beautiful within."

— Socrates

"It is a great thing to be humble when you are brought low; but to be humble when you are praised is a great and rare attainment."

— St. Bernard

"God opposes the proud, but gives grace to the humble."

— James 4:6b NIV

"In matters of principle, stand like a rock; in matters of taste, swim with the current. Give up money, give up fame, give up science, give up the earth itself and all it contains, rather than do an immoral act. And never suppose, that in any possible situation, or under any circumstances, it is best for you to do a dishonorable thing. Whenever you are to do a thing, though it can never be known but to yourself, ask yourself how would you act were all the world looking at you, and act accordingly.

"He who permits himself to tell a lie once finds it much easier to do it a second and third time, till at length it becomes habitual; he tells a lie without attending to it, and truths without the world believing him."

— Thomas Jefferson

Perseverance

"Victory belongs to the most persevering."
— Napoleon

No one goes through life without difficulties and failures. Risking failure is required to make improvement. There is no better place in a young person's life to take risks than in athletics. There should be no permanent damage done to the athlete who fails on the field or court. Athletics provides opportunities to learn, to quickly recover, and to keep your sights set on the next goal. So many young people have learned to give up easily. Others only try things that they can already accomplish and not risk any failure. Athletes must not take this approach. Coaches can promote and teach perseverance using positive coaching techniques and avoiding ever embarrassing their athletes. The power that encouraging words can have on perseverance, is best told in the following story.

A group of frogs were traveling through the woods, and two of them fell into a deep pit. All the other frogs gathered around the pit. When they saw how deep the pit was, they told the two frogs that they were as good as dead. The two frogs ignored the comments and tried to jump up out of the pit with all their might. The other frogs kept yelling at them to stop, that they were as good as dead.

Finally, one of the frogs took heed to what the other frogs were saying and gave up. He fell down and died. The other frog continued to jump as hard as he could. Once again, the crowd of frogs yelled at him to stop the pain and just die. He jumped even harder and finally, he made it out. When he got out, the other frogs said, "Did you not hear us?" The frog explained that he was deaf. He had thought that they had been encouraging him the entire time.

The story teaches two lessons:

- There is power of life and death in the tongue. A discouraging word can rob another of their spirit in difficult times.

- An encouraging word to someone who is down can lift them up and help them accomplish things that they may not otherwise accomplish.

"The man who wins may have been counted out several times, but didn't hear the referee."

— H.E. Janson

"Our greatest weakness lies in giving up. The most certain way to succeed is always to try just one more time."

— Thomas Edison

"Paralyze their resistance with your persistence."

— Woody Hayes

"Perseverance isn't just the willingness to work hard. It is that, plus the willingness to be stubborn about your belief in yourself."

— Merlin Olsen

"Start with the premise that, in general, people would rather do something less difficult than something difficult. Certain kinds of extreme circumstances demand high levels of effort. People resist giving that high level of effort. There is a tendency to settle for less and then have to overcome that."

— Pete Carill

"The brook would lose its song if you removed the rocks."

— Unknown

"Sometimes it is more important to discover what one cannot do, than what one can do."

— Lin Yutang

"The difference between a hero and an also-ran is the guy who hangs on for one last grasp."

— Paul Dietzel

"I am not what I ought to be,
Not what I want to be,
Not what I am going to be
But I am thankful that
I am better than I used to be."

— Unknown

"Difficulties in life are intended to make us better, not bitter."

— Dan Reeves

"God has not promised us a quiet journey, only a safe arrival."

— Unknown

"Face your deficiencies and acknowledge them. But do not let them master you."

— Helen Keller

"Man's greatest moment of happiness is to be tested beyond what he thought might be his breaking point and not fail."

— Joseph Murphy

"Any fool can criticize, condemn, and complain – and most fools do."
— Dale Carnegie

"Never tell a young person that something cannot be done. God may have been waiting for centuries for somebody ignorant of the impossible to do that very thing.

— J.A. Holmes
American clergyman

"Failure is the opportunity to begin again, more intelligently."

— Henry Ford

"Never let your head hang down.
Never give up and sit down and grieve.
Find another way."

— Satchel Paige

"Happiness, I have discovered, is nearly always a rebound from hard work."

— David Grayson

"Giving up reinforces our sense of incompetence; going on gives you a commitment to success."

— George Weinberg

"Sympathy is like junk food, it has no real value."

— Anonymous

"Adversity causes some men to break, and others to break records."

— Unknown

"Anyone can get good results from a physically perfect individual who is forced into a scientific training regime. The beauty comes when someone who is imperfect but has great desire and as a result achieves great results."

— Emil Zatopek
Distance runner, olympic gold medalist

"Sweet are the uses of adversity."

— Shakespeare

"Only in winter can you see which trees are truly green. Only when the winds of adversity blow can you tell whether an individual or a country has courage and steadfastness."

— John F. Kennedy

"Things that hurt, instruct."

— Ben Franklin

"The difference between the possible and impossible lies in the man's determination."

— Tommy Lasorda

"Don't let yesterday take up too much of today."

— Will Rogers

"Quitting is a cinch. You walk away. For the time being, you're the boss, you're free as a bird. When you are young, people excuse a lot of things. But when you get older, people stop feeling sorry for you and quitting isn't so popular."

— Joe Black

"I have brought myself by long meditation to the conviction that a human being with a settled goal must accomplish it, and that nothing can resist a will which will stake even existence upon it's fulfillment."

— Benjamin Disraeli

"People seldom want to walk over you until you lie down."

— Elmer Wheeler

"Everybody is looking for instant success, but it doesn't work that way. You build a successful life one day at a time."

— Lou Holtz

"Character cannot be developed in ease and quiet. Only through experiences of trial and suffering can the soul be strengthened, vision cleared, ambition inspired and success achieved."

— Helen Keller

"Try not to do too many things at once. Know what you want, the number one thing for today and tomorrow, is to persevere and get it done."

— George Allen

"The stones that critics hurl with harsh intent, a man may use to build a monument."

— Arthur Guiterman

"Our mistakes don't make or break us. If we are lucky, they simply reveal who we really are, what we're really made of. Challenges will come, but if you treat them simply as tests of who you are, you'll come out of it not bitter and victimized, but smarter and stronger."

— Donn Moomaw

"Patience is a virtue. It takes time to create excellence. If it could be done quickly, more people would do it."

— John Wooden

"When you get to the end of your rope, tie a knot and hang on."

— Franklin D. Roosevelt

"There is a correlation between sustained effort and winning."

— Anonymous

"There is nothing the body suffers which the soul may not profit by."

— George Meredith

"…let us throw off everything that hinders and the sin that so easily entangles, and let us run with perseverance the race marked out for us."

— Hebrews 12:1

"Times of general calamity and confusion have ever been productive of the greatest minds. The purest ore is produced from the hottest furnace, and the brightest thunderbolt is elicited from the darkest storm."

— Arthur Colton

"I have fought the good fight, I have finished the race, I have kept the faith. Now there is in store for me the crown of righteousness, which the Lord, the righteous judge, will award to me on that day…"

— II Timothy 4: 7-8

"Of all our troubles, great and small, the greatest are the ones that don't happen at all."

— Thomas Carlyle

"The sacrifices that are necessary to be successful, become easier when one places a goal or objective at a high level."

— Ara Parseghian

"Failure is only postponed success, as long as courage 'coaches' ambition. The habit of persistence is the habit of victory."

— Herbert Kaufman

"We get hunted down, but God never abandons us. We get knocked down, but we get up again and keep going."

— II Corinthians 4:9

Winning and Losing

"We play with enthusiasm and recklessness. We aren't afraid to lose. If we win, great. But win or lose, it is the competition that gives us pleasure."

— Joe Paterno

By its nature, athletics is structured so that winning is the goal. Everyone in athletics will face both winning and losing. How athletes learn to deal with both will determine their continued improvement, develop their humility, and provide them with the ability to see the bigger picture. Proper perspective in winning and losing must be taught and modeled. In youth sport, the effort to prepare and the desire to compete must take precedence over a comparative score. If properly taught, the scoreboard will not be the best indicator of success. Instead we must desire to reach personal and team levels of excellence when measured against your own "best self."

"The 'final score' is not the final score. My final score is how prepared you were to execute near your own particular level of compe-
tence, both individually and as a team."

— John Wooden

"Winning is the epitome of honesty."

— Woody Hayes

"Some days you are the dog, some days you are the hydrant."

— Unknown

"I pray not for victory, but to do my best."

—Amos Alonzo Stagg

"Winning isn't getting ahead of others, it is getting ahead of yourself."

—Roger Staubach

"All men can see these tactics whereby I conquer, but what none can
see is the strategy out of which victory is evolved."

— Sun Tzu

"The more successful you become, the longer the yardstick people
use to measure you by."

— Joe Paterno

"Success is best measured by the achiever."

— Joe Paterno

"Nicklaus plays in a trance. He and the club and the ball are one, and there's nothing else. He can lock right in. That's real one-pointedness. I think he can influence the ball's flight even after it's hit."

— Michael Murphy

"Don't let winning make you soft. Don't let losing make you quit. Don't let your teammates down in any situation."

— Larry Bird

"Success in life comes not from holding a good hand, but in playing a poor hand well."

— Unknown

"The way you win is to get average players to play good and good players to play great."

— Bum Phillips

"Success – it is what you do with what you've got."

— Woody Hayes

"He who swells in prosperity will shrink in adversity."

— Anonymous

"One thing I do not like about losing is the winkers. They don't know what to say, so they wink."

— Tom Cahill

"We, on our side, are praying to Him to give us victory, because we believe we are right; but those on the other side pray to Him too, for victory, believing they are right. What must He think of us?"

— Abraham Lincoln

"Success isn't something that just happens – success is learned, success is practiced and then it is shared."

— Sparky Anderson

"Don't be afraid to fail. Experience is just mistakes you don't make anymore."

— Joe Garagiola

"Losers never know why they are losing. They will mention injuries, the officiating, the weather and bad breaks."

— George Allen

"A man who suffers before it is necessary, suffers more than is necessary."

— Seneca

"All quitters are good losers."

— Bob Zuppke

"You cannot win a battle in any arena merely by defending yourself."

— Richard Nixon

"Losing is only temporary and not all encompassing. You must simply study it, learn from it, and try hard not to lose the same way again. Then you must have the self-control to forget about it."

— John Wooden

"Once a match is over, it's over. I don't carry either the pain or the glory with me for very long."

— Bjorn Borg

"When I was losing, they called me nuts. When I was winning, they called me eccentric."

— Al McGuire

"Many times, the best way to learn is through mistakes. A fear of making mistakes can bring individuals to a standstill, to a dead center. Fear is the wicked wand that transforms human beings into vegetables."

— George Brown

"A life of frustration is inevitable for any coach whose main enjoyment is winning."

— Chuck Noll

Bum Phillips reviewing a game after a loss:
"The film looks suspiciously like the game itself."

"Failure is an event, never a person."

> **— William D. Brown**

"Success is never final. Failure is never fatal."

> **— Joe Paterno**

"In warfare, there are no constant conditions. He who can modify his tactics in relation to his opponent will succeed and win."

> **— Sun-Tzu**

"Success is measured by your discipline and inner peace."

> **— Mike Ditka**

"Winning and losing are both very temporary things. Having done one or the other, you move ahead. Gloating over a victory or sulking over a loss is a good way to stand still."

> **— Chuck Knox**

"If you keep doing things the way you have always done them, you will keep getting whatever you have gotten."

> **— Unknown**

"Success is to be measured not so much by the position one has reached in life, as by the obstacles he or she has overcome while trying to succeed."

— Booker T. Washington

"How a man plays the game shows something of his character; how he loses shows all of it."

— Frosty Westering

"It isn't hard to be good from time to time in sports. What is tough, is being good every day."

— Willie Mays

"The wonderful thing about the game of life is that winning and losing are only temporary--- unless you quit."

— Unknown

"In great attempts it is glorious even to fail."

— Wilfred A. Peterson

"Before you can win a game, you must first not lose it."

— Chuck Noll

"The taste of defeat has a richness of experience all its own."

— Bill Bradley

"Nothing is wrong with losing unless you learn to accept it."

— Paul Brown

"You are never really playing an opponent. You are playing yourself, your own highest standards, and when you reach your limits, that is real joy."

— Arthur Ashe

"Failure to hit the bull's-eye is never the fault of the target. To improve your aim, improve yourself."

— Arland Gilbert

"Without winners, there would be no civilization."

— Woody Hayes

"The height of human desire is what wins, whether it's on the Normandy Beach or in Ohio Stadium."

— Woody Hayes

"In war, there is no substitute for victory."

— General Douglas MacArthur

"If you insist on measuring yourself, put a tape around your heart rather than your head."

— Anonymous

"Aggressive play is a vital asset of the world's greatest golfers. However, it is even more important to the average player. Attack this game in a bold, confident, and determined way, and you'll make a giant leap toward realizing your full potential as a player."

— Greg Norman

"Never go to bed a loser."

— sign in George Halas' office

"The best way to double your money is to fold it over and put it back in your pocket."

— Unknown

"The more difficult the victory, the greater the happiness in winning."

— Pele

"I celebrate a victory when I start walking off the field. By the time I get to the locker room, I'm done."

— Tom Osborne

"Tough years, losses and setbacks will not block the vision of a person that is self-motivated. A squad made up of these type players will not jump ship on you. They will not be blinded. They will keep driving until they start receiving the rewards of their efforts."

— Dick Vermeil

"Everyone wants to work for you when you win. Everyone wants to be your best friend when you win. The real test comes when you lose."

— **Dick Vermeil**

"I believe that people who say that winning isn't important are people who haven't won at anything."

— **Reebok commercial**

"To win, you have to risk loss."

— **Jean-Claude Killy**

"When I lose, I take my losses hard. It's my prerogative. But when my team works hard, no matter what the score, I am with them."

— **Pete Carill**

Recruiting: "You can't win with three-car garage guys. With two-car garage guys you've got a chance. I was a no-car garage guy in a $21 a-month apartment."

— **Pete Carill**

"Winning is the science of being totally prepared."

— **George Allen**

"Success requires more backbone than wishbone."

— **Unknown**

"The successful man lengthens his stride when he discovers that the signpost has deceived him; the failure looks for a place to sit down."

— J. R. Rogers

"Man's finest hour is the moment when he has worked his heart out in a good cause and lies exhausted on the field of battle – victorious."

— Vince Lombardi

"General Custer was a wild-eyed underestimater of his opponents' strength and skill."

— Wisdom Of the Elders

"You can't cross the sea merely by staring at the water."

— Rabindranath Tagore

"We compete, not so much against an opponent, but against ourselves. The real test is this: Did I make my best effort on every play?"

— Bud Wilkinson

"Even to lose, I think I'd still compete. No matter how it goes or how I go, I wouldn't change anything. It fulfills me to be able to compete. I never worry about winning or losing because when you compete, you are already a winner."

— Daley Thompson

"Shallow men believe in luck... strong men believe in cause and effect."

— Emerson

"If you don't invest much of yourself, then defeat doesn't hurt very much and winning isn't very exciting."

— Dick Vermeil

"The biggest opponent of success is not failure, it is mediocrity."

— Unknown

"Failures are expected by losers, ignored by winners."

— Joe Gibbs

"Winning is overemphasized. The only time it is important is in surgery and war."

— Al McGuire

"The man who makes the first bad move always loses the game."

— Japanese proverb

"How much does he gain, who learns when he loses."

— Italian proverb

Discipline

"What we do upon some great occasion will probably depend on what we already are; and what we are will be the result of previous years of self-discipline."

— H.P. Liddo

Discipline is a positive term and personal characteristic. Discipline is a choice. Disciplined athletes accomplish more, have a greater sense of pride and tend to be exceptional teammates. They are reliable, and trustworthy. Having discipline is essential to being "coachable". Athletes who are disciplined can take correction as a compliment because they understand that the coach's job is to identify areas of weakness and help them improve. They also equate correction as the coach seeing potential in them to get better. Discipline involves learning to respect the game, their teammates, the coach and most of all, themselves. They show this type of discipline by demonstrating directed effort and attention. Once discipline is learned by athletes, they can carry that ability to every situation they face outside of sports.

For coaches, developing positive discipline is finding the correct balance between work and fun. All work becomes forced labor, and all fun is simply unproductive silliness. The best perspective of discipline as a coach is an approach to performing your responsibilities that emphasizes productive, purposeful teaching undertaken with both control and enjoyment.

For the team, discipline is the characteristic that sets them apart and gives them an edge. That edge is called pride. Pride is never felt by poorly disciplined teams made up of selfish individuals who play carelessly and without passion. Pride is reserved for those special teams that can accept discipline as love and can learn to apply it in their own lives.

When it comes to the attitude and effort of your athletes, discipline should be demanded in direct proportion to amount of love you have for your athletes and the game you coach.

"Discipline is part of the will. A disciplined person is one who follows the will of the one who gives the orders. You teach discipline by doing it over and over, by repetition and rote, especially in a game like football when you have very little time to decide what you are going to do. So what you do is react almost instinctively, naturally. You have done it so many times, over and over and over again."

— Vince Lombardi

"Discipline is:
Knowing what to do
Knowing when to do it
Doing it to the best of your abilities
Doing it that way every single time."

— Bob Knight

"Discipline is not a dirty word."

— Pat Riley

"The really free person in society is the one who is disciplined. Players feel loved when they are disciplined."

— Dean Smith

"Each of us has been put on earth with the ability to do something well. We cheat ourselves and the world if we don't use that ability as best we can."

— George Allen

"I believe in discipline. You can forgive incompetence. You can forgive lack of ability. But one thing you cannot ever forgive is lack of discipline."

— **Forrest Gregg**

"If you let social activities take precedence over your academic activities, then you will soon lose your basketball activities."

— **John Wooden**
to his team

"Peace of mind produces right values, right values produce right thoughts. Right thoughts produce right actions, and right actions produce work which will be a material reflection for others to see of the serenity at the center of it all."

— **Robert Pirsig**
Zen and the Art
of Motorcycle Maintenance

"Without self-discipline, success is impossible, period."

— **Lou Holtz**

"Be an active participant in your own rescue."

— **Unknown**

"The sterner the discipline, the greater the devotion."

— **Pete Carill**

"Playing intelligently means knowing when not to think. Being intelligent means behaving wisely, with discipline."

— Pete Carill

"If my players work hard every day, then they won't have to worry about game plans, or where they play, or whom they play, or about rankings and so on. They have their daily behavior – their discipline – to fall back on."

— Pete Carill

"The strength of my Princeton teams has always been attitude, intelligence and discipline."

— Pete Carill

"You beat fatigue by superior conditioning, discipline and mental toughness that will allow you to be more alert to the world around you than your competitors are."

— Steven Hannant

Great Competitors - Warriors

"So live your life that the fear of death can never enter your heart. Show respect to all people, bow to none. Sing your death song and die like a hero going home."

— Tecumseh

If you are fortunate in your coaching career, you will the privilege of having some "great ones". There are some common traits among the "great ones" we coach. There are some characteristics that make them special. They possess the mental toughness that allows them to remain confident, enthusiastic, positive, and not be swayed by temporary setbacks. Warriors have enough confidence and inner strength to stand alone with their beliefs, at the moment of truth. There is fire in them, a determination and pride to not just compete, but to excel. They are self-starters, committed to excellence, with a burning desire to go beyond "good", not embarrassed to admit that they want to be the best, unafraid of failure and not apologizing for trying to win. They love the arena and look forward to the toughest competition as a test of themselves. When they do win, they do it unselfishly with class and dignity. They let the intensity of their effort and will speak.

These players either may be gifted with exceptional physical talent or may be the "unknown" players on your teams, because they are average in skill level. But regardless of God-given physical ability, they possess the character traits that make them special to coach and that will carry them successfully through life. The characteristics of the warrior are a reflection of who they become as a person.

As I write this introductory section, I simply think about the warriors I have coached. Those athletes who are warriors know who they are (even without me ever saying a word). They have become a valued part of my personal history as a coach and the teammates with whom they have played. They represent the very best of athletic tradition.

"You are in the presence of a true competitor when you observe that he or she is indeed getting the most joy out of the most difficult circumstances. The real competitors love a tough situation. That is when they focus better and function better. their competitive greatness"

— John Wooden

"The challenge of the true warrior is to be brave and at the same time gentle."

— Unknown

"To fight and conquer in all your battles is not supreme excellence. Supreme excellence consists in breaking the enemy's resistance without fighting."

— Sun-Tzu

A warrior didn't try to stand out from the band of warriors. He strove to act bravely and honorably, to help the group in whatever way he could to accomplish its mission. If glory befell him, he was obligated to give away his most prized possessions to relatives, friends and the poor.

— Lacota Sioux

"I am not concerned with your liking me or disliking me....
All I ask is that you respect me as a human being."

— Jackie Robinson

"We are doing this because the American fans are just beginning to understand that a sport, to be a real sport, has got to be contested on the basis of the best man or team, winning – and the best has got nothing to do with how much brown or red or yellow tint is in a man's skin.

> — **Branch Rickey**
> (upon signing Jackie Robinson to a contract with the Dodgers)

"I am a Shawnee. My forefathers were warriors. Their son is a warrior. From my tribe I take nothing. I am my own fortune."

> — **Tecumseh**

"The tougher and closer the competition, the more I enjoy golf. Winning by easy margins may offer other kinds of satisfaction, but it's not nearly as enjoyable as battling it out shot by shot right down to the wire."

> — **Jack Nicklaus**

"Guts win more games than ability."

> — **Bob Zuppke**

"I fought for my people and my country. When we conquered, I remained silent as a warrior should."

> — **Rain-in-the-Face**
> Sioux

"What you have, give. Because what you save, you lose forever."

> — **Brant Ust**

"Every person should expect a little good luck and a little bad luck. I've had more than my share of the good, so when some of the other kind began coming my way, I couldn't very well moan about it."

— Roy Campanella

"I've earned respect thanks to basketball. And I'm not here just to hand it to the next person. Day in and day out, I see people take on that challenge, to take what I have earned. I've got something that people want. And I don't ever want to give it away. Whenever the time comes when I'm not able to do that, I'll just back away from the game."

— Michael Jordan

"It kills me to lose. If I'm a troublemaker – and I don't think that my temper makes me one – then it's only because I can't stand losing. That's the way I am about winning. All I ever wanted to do was finish first."

— Jackie Robinson

"The one strongest, most important idea in my game of golf – my cornerstone – is that I want to be the best. I wouldn't accept anything less than that. My ability to concentrate and work toward a goal has been my greatest asset."

— Jack Nicklaus

"A good day to fight. A good day to die!"

— Crazy Horse

"I had speed, a punch and courage – either win or die."

— Jack Dempsey

"Do you know what my favorite part of the game is? The opportunity to play. It's as simple as that. God, I love that opportunity."

— Mike Singletary

"When they treat you bad, you just got to take care of your pride, no matter what."

— Satchel Paige

"Avoid what is strong and attack what is weak. Water shapes its course according to the nature of the ground over which it flows. The warrior works out his victory in relation to the foe he is facing.

— Sun-Tzu

"When I was in the batter's box, I felt sorry for the pitcher."

— Roger Hornsby

"When I was going good, there was nothing they could do except walk me."

— Willie Mays

"In the end, the game comes down to one thing: man against man. May the best man win."

— Sam Huff

"I found this sandbank by the Pearl River near my hometown, Columbia, Mississippi. I laid out a course of 65 yards or so. Sixty-five yards on sand is like 120 on turf. But running on sand helps you make your cuts at full speed. I try to pick the heat of the day to run in, but sometimes that sand will get so hot you can't stand in one place. It'll blister your feet. You get to the point where you have to keep pushing yourself. You stop, throw up, and push yourself again. There's no one around to feel sorry for you,"

— Walter Payton

"Men die of fright and live by confidence."

— Thoreau

"Be at your best when your best is needed."

— Tyler Benson

"Don't tell me how rough the waters are. Just bring the ship in."

— Chuck Knox

"I bow to no man for I am considered a prince among my people. I will gladly shake your hand."

— Joseph Brant
Mohawk (to King George III)

"When you step on the field, you cannot concede a thing."

— Gayle Sayers

"When two athletes are equal in natural ability, preparation, conditioning, concentration and confidence, who will win? The athlete with the most pride. No matter what happens, never let them take your pride."

— Peter Brousseau

"The important thought is that the Packers thrived on tough competition. We welcomed it; the team had always welcomed it. The adrenalin flowed a little quicker when we were playing the tougher teams."

— Vince Lombardi

"My goal is to be recognized as the best. No doubt about it. When they say middle linebacker from now on, I want them to mean Butkus."

— Dick Butkus

"If you want to be the person you ought to be, you've got to welcome competition."

— Bob Richards

"Enjoy the tough battle. A warrior doesn't beg, cry, alibi, sulk or lose self control."

— Anthony Giles

"Fortune favors the bold."

— Virgil

"When I'd get tired and want to stop, I'd wonder what my next opponent was doing. I'd wonder if he was still working out. I tried to visualize him. When I could see him still working, I'd start pushing myself. When I could see him in the shower, I'd push myself harder."

— Dan Gable

"If you want to see a great fighter at his best, watch him when he is getting beat."

— Sugar Ray Robinson

"My ambition is not to be just a good fighter, I want to be great, something special."

— Sugar Ray Leonard

"Everyone knows I don't have a knockout punch. I just keep coming on strong. Put King Kong in front of me and I'll still keep coming until I knock him out."

— Sugar Ray Leonard

"I like to train. I enjoy challenges, but most of all, I like winning."

— Sugar Ray Leonard

"Be a little against fighting, but when someone shoots, be ready for battle."

— Sitting Bull

"To be a winner, you've got to be bigger than the weather."

— Vince Lombardi

"I always set out to deliberately wear down the man who was covering me. I felt confident that when I was still relatively fresh, he was bound to be tiring."

— John Havlicek

When his manager suggested that he sit out the last game of the season to preserve his .400 batting average, Ted Williams chose to play. "I'm going to play. I don't want to slip into the .400 circle through the back door. I don't care to known as the .400 hitter with a lousy average of .39955. If I'm going to be a .400 hitter, I want to have more than my toenails on the line."

— Ted Williams

"Only a man who knows what it is like to be defeated can reach down to the bottom of his soul and come up with the extra ounce of power it takes to win when the match is even."

— Muhammad Ali

"I hated every minute of training, but I said, 'Don't quit. Suffer now and live the rest of your life as a champion."

— Muhammad Ali

"Being cold, like being determined to win, is just a state of mind."

— Woody Hayes

"I've always made a total effort, even when the odds seemed entirely against me. I never quit trying; I never felt I didn't have a chance to win."

— Arnold Palmer

"My idea was to do everything better than anybody else ever had. I concentrated on every aspect of the game."

— Willie Mays

"The good fighter, first puts himself beyond the possibility of defeat and then waits for the opportunity to defeat his enemy."

— Sun-Tzu

"In the closing seconds of every game, I want the ball in my hands for that last shot — not in anybody else's, not in anybody else's hands in the world."

— Larry Bird

"He was like an untrained or untouched horse, wild, ignorant of domestic uses, splendid in action and unconscious of danger."

— Two Strike
Tashunkekokipapi – Sioux
(speaking about Crazy Horse)

"What I'm waiting for is a game where I don't miss a tackle, where I and everyone around me do everything to the absolute letter of perfection. I do have that game in my repertoire and until that time, I will not be fulfilled."

— Joe Greene

"For your bravery on the battlefields and as the greatest warrior of our bands, we have elected you as our war chief, leader of the entire Sioux nation. When you tell us to fight, we shall fight; when you tell us to make peace, we shall make peace."

— **Four Horns**
(speaking to Sitting Bull)

"You ought to run the hardest when you feel the worst. Never let the other guy know you're down."

— **Joe Dimaggio**

"Make your opponent respect your will to win."

— **Curtis Borchardt**

"Mental toughness is many things. It is humility because it behooves all of us to remember that simplicity is the sign of greatness, and meekness is the sign of true strength. Mental toughness is spartanism with the qualities of sacrifice, self-denial, dedication. It is fearlessness, and it is love."

— **Vince Lombardi**

The grandfather of American Horse at his birth:

"Put him out in the sun! Let him ask his great grandfather, the Sun, for the warm blood of a warrior."

"From now until the end of time, no one else will ever see life with my eyes, and I mean to make the most of my chance."

— Christopher Morley

"True success is one of our greatest needs. Success is not something you stumble onto or come to by accident. It is something you must sincerely prepare for. Take a good look at successes, and you'll see the same consistent qualities all the time – qualities of one's character that make one strive for a goal with a standard of unmatched excellence."

— Reggie Jackson

"Should my blood be sprinkled, I want no wounds from behind. Death should come fronting me."

— Toohoohoolzote
Nez Perce chief

"Nothing is so strong as gentleness; nothing so gentle as real strength."

— St. Francis de Salis

"In a race, everyone runs, but only one person gets first prize... run your race to win. Everyone who competes in the games goes into strict training. They do it to get a crown that will not last; but we do it to get a crown that will last forever."

— I Corinthians 9:24

"Nobody who ever gave their best effort regretted it."

— George Halas

"A lot of people run a race to see who is fastest. I run to see who has the most guts, who can push himself into an exhausting pace and then at the end, punish himself even more. Nobody is going to win a 5,000-meter race after running an easy two miles. Not with me. If I lose forcing the pace all the way, well at least I can live with myself."

— Steve Prefontaine

"Great men are meteors designed to burn so that the earth may be lighted."

— Napoleon

"Two things that are never said about true champions: Our opponents wanted the game more than we did, or they were more ready to play the game than we were."

— Don Shula

"There comes a time, when the game or season is on the line, when you have to block out the pain and contribute whatever you can. There is no way they are going to play the last game without me"

— Willis Reed

"Just play the thing out. Play until there's no time left to play."

— Todd Blackledge

"It is how you show up at the showdown that counts."

— Homer Norton

"One of man's finest qualities is described by the simple word 'guts' – the ability to take it. If you have the discipline to stand when your body wants to run, if you can control your temper and remain cheerful in the face of monotony or disappointment, you have 'guts' in the soldiering sense."

— John S. Roosma

"Coolness and a steady nerve will always beat simple quickness. Take your time and you'll only have to pull the trigger once."

— Anonymous

"Most things that were once believed impossible are now commonplace."

— Unknown

"Every game is an opportunity to measure yourself against your own potential."

— Bud Wilkinson

Confidence

"Confidence comes from being prepared."

— John Wooden

Confidence that benefits our athletes in all areas of their life is an inner confidence, based on preparation to perform well. It is a quiet confidence that calms and relaxes the performer and allows them to concentrate and visualize a positive effort.

Teaching confidence to young athletes often begins with breaking down the images of arrogance that are so often represented by professional athletes in the media. Confidence is not self-centeredness or bragging. It is not trying to anticipate the outcome of a game ("I think we'll kick their butt"). The extent that the athlete can separate anticipated outcome and confidence based on their own preparation may determine how well they play.

True confidence provides the athlete and team with an opportunity to enter into competition feeling that they will perform well by focusing on their own practices and what they have control over, without factoring in the opponent. Knowing that they are prepared and ready for anything that may happen in competition allows athletes to recover from temporary setbacks and carry themselves with poise in all situations.

During the practices leading up to a game, we continually refocus our teams by asking them if they are preparing well enough to leave them feeling totally prepared. At the conclusion of the last practice prior to a game, we try to get our athletes to build true confidence by focusing back on the days of preparation and by asking them for reasons "why they think they will play well as an individual and as a team". This step places the emphasis where it should be — on our team, our practices and our preparation, and not on factors over which we have no control.

"I've always thought I could do whatever was necessary to succeed."

— **Michael Jordan**

"My religious beliefs teach me to feel as safe in battle as in bed."

— **Stonewall Jackson**

"You don't aim at the bullseye. You aim at the center of the bullseye."

— **Raymond Berry**

"Valor and confidence grow by being daring; fear and failure by holding back."

— **Unknown**

"If you can't bite, don't show your teeth."

— **Yiddish Proverb**

"God gives the shoulder according to the burden."

— **German Proverb**

"If I make a mistake, I'm going to make a mistake aggressively, and I'm going to make it quickly. I don't believe in sleeping on a decision."

— **Bo Schembechler**

"I sought advice and cooperation from all those around me – but not permission."

— Mohammad Ali

"The greatest pleasure in life is doing what people say that you cannot do."

— Walter Bagehot

"The length of the conversation don't tell nothing about the size of the intellect."

— Unknown

"It often shows a fine command of language to say nothing."

— Unknown

"Athletes, as with all people, fall into two motivational categories: those that truly want success and those who simply try to avoid failure."

— Eric Hanson

"Nothing can shake my self-confidence. When you reach a certain level, you never experience the slightest anxiety. There's never the slightest apprehension."

— Jean-Claude Killy

"Egotism is the anesthetic that deadens the pain of stupidity."

— Knute Rockne

"A man need not extol his virtue, nor comment on his failings. His friends know the former, and his enemies will search out the latter."

— Charles A. Rogers

"A man is always better than he thinks he is."

— Woody Hayes

"It is never an upset if the so-called underdog has all along considered itself the better team."

— Woody Hayes

"If your mind isn't clouded with unnecessary things, this is the best season of your life."

— Wu-Men

"It is no great thing to be humble when you are brought low; but to be humble when you are praised is a great and rare achievement."

— St. Bernard
Italian Bishop

"Each one should test his own actions. Then he can take pride in himself, without comparing himself to somebody else."

— Galatians 6:4 NIV

"I can't stand a ballplayer who plays in fear. Any fellow who has a good shot has got to take it and keep taking it. So he misses – so what?"

— **Red Auerbach**

"The biggest mistake an athlete can make is to be afraid to make one."

— **L. Ron Hubbard**
American author

"A man wrapped up in himself, makes a very small bundle."

— **Benjamin Franklin**

"You don't need to decorate your words to make them clear. Say it plain and save some breath for breathin'."

— **Anonymous**

"If you say what you think, you are considered cocky or conceited. But if you have an objective in life, you shouldn't be afraid to stand up and say it. In second grade, they asked us what we wanted to be. I said I wanted to be a ballplayer, and they laughed. In the eighth grade they asked the same question, and I said a ballplayer, and they laughed a little more. By the eleventh grade, no one was laughing."

— **Johnny Bench**

"A good mind has never handicapped a player."

— **Pete Carill**

"There is a difference between conceit and confidence. A quarterback has to have confidence. Conceit is bragging about yourself. Confidence means you believe you can get the job done. I have always believed that I could get the job done."

— Johnny Unitas

"No one can make you feel inferior without your consent."

— Eleanor Roosevelt

"Basketball is just something else to do, another facet of life. I'm going to be a success at whatever I choose because of my preparation. By the time the game starts, the outcome has been decided. I never think about having a bad game because I have prepared."

— David Robinson

"Over the years, I've studied habits of golfers. I know what to look for. Watch their eyes. Fear shows up when there is an enlargement of the pupils. Big pupils lead to big scores."

— Sam Snead

"Empty barrels make the most noise."

— Chuck Noll,
(about a player who bragged a lot)

Poise

"If you get caught up in things over which you have no control, it will adversely affect those things over which you have control."

— Advice to John Wooden from his father

It is easy to be positive and focused when everything is going great. But an athlete who can maintain that sense of composure when things are not going well gives himself and his team the gift of poise. Being able to be at ease in any situation leads to consistent performance. The statement "the team that loses its poise will probably lose" is very true in all sports that require any measure of skill or concentration. The player that can recover quickly from mistakes is less likely to repeat them. Controlling your emotions in such a way that you become unflappable is a key ingredient in becoming a great competitor. Players who are truly mentally tough will learn that one of the results of losing their temper can be to fortify the resolve of their opponents. When athletes see that their opposition is upset, it can be energizing to them because it must surely mean that they are doing something well. By the same token, athletes and coaches should avoid showing disgust or disappointment when their teammates or players make mistakes. A person with poise is more often than not someone who offers encouragement in these situations, quickly recovering himself and helping others to do the same. In athletics, poise should be demonstrated at all times — with yourself, your teammates, your opponents, and officials.

"Poise and confidence will come from conditioning, skill, and team spirit. To have poise and be truly confident, you must be in condition and know you are fundamentally sound, and possess the proper team attitude."

— John Wooden

"Anger is just one letter short of danger."

— Unknown

"I want to always convey to my teammates and to the opposition that I am in control of myself. I don't want anyone to think that I am intimidated by anything going on out of the field."

— Mike Schmidt

"Free your mind and the rest will follow."

— En Vogue

"The masters all have the ability to discipline themselves to eliminate everything except what they are trying to accomplish.

— Dale Brown

"When you lose control of your emotions, when your self-discipline breaks down, your judgement and common sense suffer. How can you perform at your best when you are using poor judgement?"

— John Wooden

"Anger is cruel and fury is overwhelming..."

— Proverbs 27:4 NIV

"Anger is never without reason, but seldom with a good one."

— Benjamin Franklin

"The key to winning is poise under stress."

— Paul Brown

"The first rule when you are in a hole: If you are in one, stop digging."

— Unknown

"The only way to maximize potential for performance is to be calm in the mind."

— Brian Sipe

"Given an equality of strength and skill, the victory in golf will be to him who is captain of his soul."

— Arnold Haultain

"People ask me what makes a great skier. It takes the gift; but besides the gift it takes that availability of the mind which permits total control of all the elements that lead to victory – total composure."

— Jean-Claude Killy

"Humans are the only creature who, when they lose their way, run faster."

— Unknown

"There is no room in your mind for negative thoughts. The busier you keep yourself with the particulars of shot assessment and execution, the less chance your mind has to dwell on the emotional. This is sheer intensity."

— Jack Nicklaus

"A quick tempered man does foolish things…"

— Proverbs 14:17 NIV

"When it comes to celebrating, act like you've been there before."

— Terry Bowden

"Don't lose you head, it may be the best part of your body."

— Tim Stonich

"Maintain your composure. The worst thing you can do to an opponent is to defeat him."

— Paul Brown

"Poise, concentration. No indecision. No wasted motion. No strong-arm tactics. Only an easy fluid, motion. That's the secret of my game."

— Julius Boros

"There is a difference between spirit and temperament. It is a slight difference, but it is an important one. I valued players with spirit and avoided those who were temperamental."

— John Wooden

"Never bear more than one trouble at a time. Some people bear three kinds – all they have had, all they have now and all they expect to have."

— Edward Everett Hale

"When I play, I'm boiling inside. I just try not to show it because it's a lack of composure, and if you give in to your emotions after one loss, you're liable to have three or four in a row."

— Chris Evert

Sportsmanship

"One man practicing sportsmanship, is better than a hundred teaching it."
— **Knute Rockne**

The behavior of a team's players in competition is the most revealing public reflection of a coach. Like it or not, our athletes are on stage, being critiqued by all in attendance. But more important than the reaction from others is the opportunity athletics has to reveal personal character to the athlete himself. This may be the only place in young players' lives where they are under such scrutiny and have a chance to show what they have learned. Every game and every practice provide a test for each player to win or lose with class, to learn to accept decisions made by others, and to do what is right regardless of other influences.

Sportsmanship is not a passive activity of acceptance. Rather, it is a positive reaffirmation of the fact that an athlete is disciplined enough to have perspective, maintain poise, and do what is best for his teammates. Teaching your athletes to make the correct behavioral choice at the "moment of truth" is the responsibility of the coach.

As a coaching staff, we introduce sportsmanship as a theme early in the season. This character trait must be very clearly defined and monitored. As a coaching staff, you and your colleagues must decide how you want your athletes to respond to potential problem areas in your sport. Then set up learning situations in practice, before the games start, that will enable your athletes to learn how to properly deal with such scenarios. If your athletes are going to make mistakes in how they behave, it is essential that you discover this fact, and take whatever necessary corrective actions are appropriate before formal competition actually begins.

The following two examples illustrate how we tested our players in practice and taught them to respond properly according to expectations of our program:

- Bring in an official to practice and have the athletes get used to responding to various whistle and judgement calls. During this session, we occasionally ask the official to make some calls that are exactly opposite of the correct judgement. In other words, the official intentionally makes some bad calls. For example, if the blue team was the last team to touch the ball, the referee could blow his whistle and award the ball back to blue. This step provides our athletes a chance to react correctly or incorrectly to an obviously wrong call by the official. After a few minutes, we stop practice and explain what we have asked the referee to do. We then take some time to identify responses from the players that were both acceptable and unacceptable. From that point on, our players never know if calls that are being made in practice are a "set up" by the coach in order to test their reaction or simply a call with which they disagree. The lesson we're attempting to get across to our players is to play hard, listen to the call, do not try to influence it in any way and quickly recover and get back to the part of the game over which you have control.

- If we anticipate that sometime during the season we are possibly going to face a team that may play outside the rules of game, use profanity, or attempt to fight, we set up in practice what we refer to as the "walk-away drill." Before practice, we confer with a player and describe to him an unsportsmanlike act that we want him to do to a specific player. For example, in football, we would have the "set up" player go up at the conclusion of a play and shove or taunt a player on our team who may have a "short fuse." We only let it go as long as the time involved in the offended player's first reaction to the affront. Coaches are ready for this moment, stop the action; and bring the team together to explain what has just happened. Knowing that the possibility for such behavior exists from any opponent, the lesson is that if you react to poor behavior with poor behavior of your own, you will probably be the one penalized. Therefore, our team is hurt by your personal decision to respond with unsportsmanlike behavior. The only acceptable reaction is to "walk away" from trouble without any response. The true competitor can channel his aggressiveness to only come out within the rules of the game, and doesn't penalize his team by losing his poise.

Coaches should think of situations that their athletes will have to face in their specific sport that will test their sportsmanship and then create opportunities in practice that will allow them to be successful when it counts.

Sportsmanship, whether it is good or bad, cannot be hidden. It must be taught, modeled and expected from athletes and coaches. This character trait is a key component in a successful athletic experience.

"If the coach insists upon hard play, but clean play, the team will do likewise."

— Knute Rockne

"I've always felt that a champion shouldn't let things like questionable line calls bother her."

— Chris Evert

"There was never a champion who to himself was a good loser. There is a vast difference between a good sport and a good loser."

— Red Blaik

"There is no mat space for malcontents or dissenters. One must neither celebrate insanely when he wins nor sulk when he loses. He accepts victory professionally, humbly; he hates defeat, but makes no poor display of it."

— Dan Gable

"An athlete is not crowned unless he competes according to the rules."

— II Timothy 2:5

"It is good sportsmanship to not pick up a lost golf ball while it is still rolling."

— Mark Twain

Friendship

"As iron sharpens iron, so one man sharpens another."

— Proverbs 27:17

Other than with their family, most young people find their next best opportunity to learn about personal relationships with an athletic team. They are often placed with a group of people whom they may not know, and with whom they need to form a relationship based upon mutual dependence. They learn how to meet and work with people whom they have not met before and who may possess a variety of different skills, interests and backgrounds. Athletes soon discover that they have a common goal. In order to have a better chance to reach that goal, they need to build trust, respect and loyalty.

Friendships grow as teammates learn to depend on each other and when they achieve success. Development of proper work habits and perseverance builds mutual respect. Recognizing that teammates can be consistently counted on to give their best effort leads to trust. Loyalty is the result of going through tough times and passing the test together. Pride is the last step in forming friendship. In a few unique situations, a limited number of teams attain this special sense of pride, when their players combine the qualities of sincere enthusiasm, determination, intensity and conditioning, and make a personal choice to place the needs of the team ahead of themselves. Such qualities are the foundations of true friendships. Through the leadership shown by their coaches, athletes learn to identify and exhibit those qualities both on and off the field or court. As a result, they will be helped in all future relationships.

"The smallest good deed is better than the best intention."

— Anonymous

"Everyone I meet is in some way my superior."

— William Shakespeare

"Make yourself necessary to somebody."

— Ralph Waldo Emerson

"Rings and jewels are not gifts, but apologies for gifts. The only true gift is a portion of thyself."

— Ralph Waldo Emerson

"The people I feel closest to are people who don't compromise their basic nature and the way they feel."

— Dustin Hoffman

"A real friend is one who helps us to think our best thoughts, do our noblest deeds, and be our finest selves."

— Unknown

"A hug is a great gift... One size fits all, and it's easy to exchange."

— Unknown

At the conclusion of the Civil War, when told by an advisor that he should destroy his enemies rather than make friends of them, President Abraham Lincoln said, "Am I not destroying my enemies when I make a friend of them?"

"You cannot do a kindness too soon because you never know how soon it will be too late."

— Ralph Waldo Emerson

"Fault finding is like window washing. All the dirt seems to be on the other side."

— Unknown

"I always seek the good that is in people and leave the bad to Him who made mankind and knows how to round off the corners."

— Goethe

"Love of others and love of ourselves are not alternatives. On the contrary, an attitude of love toward themselves will be found in all those who are capable of loving others.

— Erich Fromm

"To be trusted is a greater compliment than to be loved."

— George MacDonald

"Choose your friends carefully. If you hang with dogs, you'll end up with fleas."

— Unknown

"Associate with people of good qualities; it is better to be alone than in bad company."

— Unknown

"Love begins with yourself. The moment you accept what you are, you awaken your capacity to receive love."

— Amrit Desai

"You can discover more about a person in an hour of play, than in a year of conversation."

— Plato

"There is a destiny that makes us brothers,
None goes his way alone.
All that we send into the lives of others,
Comes back into our own."

— Edwin Markham

"What you don't see with your eyes, don't invent with your tongue."

— Jewish proverb

"Tis not enough to help the feeble up, but to support him after."

— William Shakespeare

"Be more prompt to go to a friend in adversity than in prosperity."

— Chilo

"Kindness is the ability to love people more than they deserve."

— Unknown

"Hold yourself responsible for a higher standard than anyone else expects of you. Never excuse yourself. Never pity yourself. Be a hard master to yourself – and be lenient to everybody else."

— Henry Ward Beecher

"You never really leave a place you love. Part of it you take with you, leaving a part of yourself behind."

— Unknown

"The only safe and sure way to destroy an enemy is to make him your friend."

— Unknown

"Reckless words pierce like a sword,
but the tongue of the wise brings healing."

— Proverbs 12:18 NIV

"The critic is one who knows the price of everything and the value of nothing."

— Oscar Wilde

"I shall pass through the world but once. Any good therefore that I can show to another human being, let me do it now."

— Mahatma Gandhi

"There is nothing so rewarding as to make people realize they are worthwhile in this world."

— Bob Anderson
English Poet

"Blessed are they who have a gift of making friends, for it is one of God's best gifts. It involves many things, but above all, the power of going out of one's self, and appreciating whatever is noble and loving in another."

— Thomas Hughes

"Be polite, treat everybody nice, and take the world as you find it."

— Mother's advice
to the Selmon brothers

"The sun nurtures and vitalizes the trees and the flowers, it does so by giving away its light, but in the end, which direction do they grow?"

— Unknown

"Humility is not thinking little of yourself, rather it is simply not thinking of yourself."

— Anonymous

"At times when I am feeling low,
I hear from a friend and then
My worries start to go away
And I am on the mend.

In spite of all that doctors know,
And their studies never end,
The best cure of all when spirits fall
Is a kind note from a friend."

— John Wooden

Teamwork

Regardless of your age, the experience of being on a great team is priceless. It is something that will influence who you are for the remainder of your life. Few experiences can be as helpful in the growth of young athletes, as being part of a selfless group working toward a common goal.

Many coaches look at team spirit as an intangible thing that some teams have and others do not. It is our job to teach, promote and build this attitude, and not leave it to chance. The coach must use every bit of his creative energy to develop team spirit within his players. You must find opportunities to encourage teamwork and unselfishness everyday. When your coaching career is over, you will remember many individual players with fondness, many will remain in contact with you and some will become friends as they mature into adulthood. Though many great personal relationships are fostered through athletics, your favorite memories will be of teams. Teams that learned the lessons you were trying to teach and accomplished goals together that they could have never done by themselves.

The satisfaction of building teams and changing the lives of individual players in the process may be the most gratifying experience coaching can offer. As their leader, you have demanded commitments and a level of excellence from them that has allowed them to achieve things that they may have thought were not possible. Getting a group of people to blend together and achieve greatness is an experience unique to a few professions. Coaching is often the model for other professions as they try to bring a "team" of people toward a common goal. Look how many of the terms we have used as coaches for years are now popular in the business world as businesses attempt to create a productive and cohesive atmosphere in the workplace.

Teams are relatively fragile and need to be constantly monitored and molded. A wise and creative coach will use everything in his power to provide a "team experience" for his players, and then once accomplished, give them proprietorship of the team.

Among the ideas that can help you develop a "team" are the following:

- Identify the team qualities you are looking for in each player and then use them as part of your squad selection criteria.

- Identify selfishness as an unacceptable behavior and eliminate it. Work to change selfish players. On the other hand, if these players do not respond to your efforts, remember that the team comes first.

- Once players have individually accepted the team standards and ethics, show and communicate how much you value these athletes regardless of specific competitive outcomes.

- Provide and promote common bonds, unifying goals, and opportunities to overcome common hardships.

- Create ways to demonstrate public and physical signs of unity.

- Work hard to find a role for every player on the team and praise each role equally. Give players an identity. Help them understand that each role contributes to team success.

- Use "spotlighting" to reinforce players who have made personal sacrifices for the betterment of the team. Continually attempt to catch those players who engage in the act of doing something well. Verbally praise and encourage their actions.

- Reward all efforts toward team play.

- Provide a stable, working environment with clear guiding principles and consistent routines and rewards.

Great teams are made up of athletes who have given up their quest for individual glory, who have willingly and wholeheartedly accepted the character traits of a team player and who have fully committed themselves to the group effort. This is a coach's greatest legacy.

"The power of we, is stronger than the power of me."

— Unknown

"You must learn how to hold a team together. You must lift some men up, calm others down, until finally they've got one heartbeat. Then you've got yourself a team."

— Bear Bryant

"The main ingredient of stardom is the rest of the team."

— Anonymous

"Success is spelled 'teamwork.' The successful teamworker doesn't have a chip on his shoulder, doesn't look for slights, isn't constantly on the alert, lest his 'dignity' be insulted. He puts the good of the house – the company or team – first. And if the whole prospers, he, as an active effective, progressive part of it, will also prosper with it."

— B.C. Forbes

"I ran my team pretty much like I ran my family. Only with my family, I had the greatest co-coach working along side of me."

— John Wooden

"I feel I've had a consistent career, but I could only be as good as the team. Contrary to what some people think, I didn't just get good again in 1981. It was no comeback. The team just got better."

— Ken Anderson

"Few burdens are heavy when everyone lifts."

— **Unknown**

"Teams can lose individual games, or even have low periods during a career, but you can always tell people who will eventually win. They have the ability to motivate themselves."

— **Unknown**

"I have seen that in any great undertaking, it is not enough for a man to depend simply upon himself."

— **Lone Man**
Teton Sioux

"Selfishness is the only real atheism; aspiration, unselfishness, the only real religion."

— **Iraeli Zangwill**

"Teamwork is the essence of life."

— **Anonymous**

"Commitment to the team – there is no such thing as in-between, you are either in or out."

— **Pat Riley**

"We teach our men that a teammate is the most important thing. I may be mad at a player, but I applaud... I will never embarrass a young man publicly."

— Dean Smith

"No person was ever honored for what he received. Honor has been the reward for what he gave."

— Calvin Coolidige

"The greatest joy one can have is doing something for someone else, without any thought of getting something in return."

— John Wooden

"My whole life, my dream was to be part of something special. I never really had any interest in being a star. I just wanted to play on a great team."

— Bill Walton

"Play for your own self-respect and the respect of your teammates."

— Dan McGugin

"A giant may conquer many, but many as one, can conquer a giant."

— Anonymous

"The strength of the wolf is in the pack, and the strength of pack is in the wolf."

— Rudyard Kipling

"The first thing any coaching staff must do is to weed out selfishness. No program can be successful with players who put themselves ahead of the team."

— Johnny Majors

"Everything on the earth has a purpose – every person a mission."

— Mourning Dove— Salish

"Loyalty is very important when things get a little tough, as they often do when the challenge is great. Loyalty is a powerful force in producing one's individual best and more so in producing a team's best."

— John Wooden

"The one-man team is a complete and total myth."

— Don Shula

"One finger cannot lift a pebble."

— Hopi saying

"Team guts always beats individual greatness."

— Bob Zuppke

Selfishness: The Cold Within

"Six men were trapped by circumstances in bleak and bitter cold
Each one possessed a stick of wood, or so the story's told.
The dying fire in need of logs, the first man held his back,
because of the faces round the fire, he noticed one was black.
The second man saw not one of the own local church,
And couldn't bring himself to give the first his stick of birch.
The poor man sat in tattered clothes and gave his coat a hitch.
Why should he give up his log to warm the idle rich?
The rich man sat and thought of all the wealth he had in store,
and how to keep what he had earned from the lazy, shiftless poor.
The black man's face spoke revenge, and the fire passed from his sight.
Because he saw in his stick of wood a chance to spite the white.
The last man of this forlorn group did not except for gain,
only to those who gave to him and how he played the game.
Their logs held tight in death's still hands was proof of human sin.
They didn't die from the cold without,
they died from The Cold Within."
— Author Unknown

"Selfishness always brings it's own revenge. It cannot be escaped. Be unselfish. It is the first and final commandment for those who would be useful and happy in their usefulness."

— Charles W. Eliott

"What I spent, I had; What I kept, I lost; What I gave, I have."

— Henry Ward Bucher

"All who exalt themselves will be humbled, and all who humble themselves will be exalted."

— Matthew 23:12

"Great teamwork is the only way to reach our ultimate moments, and create breakthroughs that define our careers and fulfill our lives."

— Pat Riley

"Anyone can support a team that is winning – it takes no courage. But to stand behind a team to defend a team when it is down and really needs you, that takes a lot of courage."

— Bart Starr

"If a team is to reach its potential, each player must willingly subordinate his own personal goals to the good of the team."

— Bud Wilkinson

" I don't know what your destiny will be, but this I know: The only ones among you who will be truly happy are those who will have sought and found how to serve."

— Albert Schweitzer

"Ten strong horses could not pull an empty baby carriage if they worked independently of each other."

— John Wooden

"Regardless of his personal accomplishments, the only true satisfaction a player receives is the satisfaction that comes from being part of a successful team."

— Vince Lombardi

"Try to forget yourself in the service of others. For when we think too much of ourselves and our own interests, we easily become despondent. But when we work for others, our efforts return to bless us."

— Sidney Powell

"The essence of the game is the soul-satisfying awareness that comes from communal work and sacrifice."

— Red Blaik

"The secret of winning football games is working more as a team, less as individuals. I play not my eleven best, but my best eleven."

— Knute Rockne

"I've never known anyone so loyal. If you are Larry Bird's teammate, you are one of the most important people in the world to him."

— Kevin McHale

"The doer makes mistakes. The team that makes the most mistakes will probably win."

— Piggy Lambert

"Individual commitment to a group effort – that is what makes a team work, a company work, a society work, and civilization work."

— Vince Lombardi

"There is one key point about picking the so-called 'great athlete'. It doesn't mean a thing if he doesn't perform with the team in mind."

— John Madden

"Plans fail for lack of counsel, but with many advisors they succeed."

— Isaiah 28:29 NIV

"People acting together as a group can accomplish things which no individual acting alone could ever hope to bring about."

— Franklin D. Roosevelt

"All of us are team players. Whether we know it or not, our significance arrives through our vital connections to other people. Family life is the central team experience."

— Pat Riley

"Without sacrifice, you will never know your teams' potential, or your own."

— Pat Riley

"The team is the star, never an individual player."

— John Wooden

"I'm convinced that a team of good character will win the close games and come through in the clutch and perform well in any circumstance."

— Terry Bradshaw

"The more honor and self-respect among players, the greater the team."

— Frosty Westering

"There is that interdependence and that strength you get from a team, that the group is greater than any individual."

— Pete Newell

Part III:
Specific Sports
and Humor

Basketball

"Bad shooters are always open."

— Pete Carill

"I first realized how much I loved the game of basketball, when I began to look forward to practices. I mean, I enjoy the practices as much as the games. Money is nothing to me. The bottom line is that I'm playing. I have a 'love of the game' clause in my contract, that allows me to play basketball any time I want during the off-season."

— Michael Jordan

"I have two college degrees, four honorary doctorate degrees, and am in three Halls of Fame, and the only thing I know how to do is teach tall people how to put a ball in a hole."

— Red Auerbach

"The best way to build team chemistry is the way Rupp used to substitute, when they fouled out."

— Dean Smith

"I've always believed in quickness over strength and size."

— Dean Smith

"Basketball is a complex dance that requires shifting from one objective to another at lightning speed. To excel, you need to act with a clear mind and be totally focused."

— Phil Jackson

"I don't have any tricky plays, I'd rather have tricky players."

— Abe Lemons

"People say to me: 'Oh we'll be happy as long as you keep bringing in fine young men to represent the university.' But I don't want to test them by going 7-20."

— Dean Smith

"My first year as a head coach, I was 29, and scared to death. I told my team about the tired signal. Four or five times the first half a player gave it to me. I thought they were saying 'We're getting them, Coach.' I had forgotten my own signal."

— Dean Smith

"I only use statistics to reinforce what I already think, or if it's something unusual."

— Dean Smith

"The key statistic is still to get to the foul line."

— Dean Smith

"As soon as we had the lead, I knew there wasn't any way we could lose. He was our Goose Gossage."

> **— Dean Smith**
> (on Phil Ford)

"As a player, remember that the bench is not a prison but an extension of the first group. Concentrate on the quality of your play when you do get into the game. If you play 20 minutes, play the best 20 minutes you can possibly play."

> **— Stan Albeck**

"Basketball is a game of conditioning and fatigue. If you don't have stamina, you'll never have the presence of mind to exercise judgement."

> **— Unknown**

"I don't recruit players who are nasty to their parents. I look for players who realize the world doesn't revolve around them."

> **— Pete Carill**

"I never substitute just to substitute. I play my regulars. The only way a guy gets off the floor is if he dies."

> **— Abe Lemons**

"We have a great bunch of outside shooters, unfortunately all of our games are played indoors."

> **— Weldon Drew**

"The greatest ally you have to get things working well and the players performing as a team is the bench. Don't be afraid to use it, either for the star player or anyone else."

— John Wooden

"I would never recruit a player who yells at his teammates, disrespected his high school coach, or scores 33 points a game and his team goes 10-10"

— Dean Smith

"Basketball has done a lot for racial justice."

— Dean Smith

"If you have all five players competing for the ball it makes them easier for the defense to guard them."

— Pete Carill

"Sometimes everything falls into place, and it's an incredible feeling. We have several players who can carry the team for part of a game. The amazing thing is that we are able recognize this. And I'll tell you something, we all get the same satisfaction out of it. We're all having fun. Working together is fun. Winning is fun. Heck, just playing is fun."

— Joe Dumars

"This is a simple game. The ball is round, and the floor is smooth."

— Red Auerbach

To a player not giving his best in practice: "The inner circle is all that matters in basketball."

— Phil Jackson

"I'm not a good recruiter. I've never been one to talk a guy into signing. I don't want to talk him into signing. I want him to select us."

— Dean Smith

"The team on the court is the team of the moment. When the first string snaps, motivate the players you have, rather than moaning about the players you don't have."

— Pat Riley

"Seven things to do: Be true to yourself; help others; make each day a masterpiece; drink deeply from great books, especially the Bible; make friendship a fine art; build a shelter against a rainy day; pray for guidance and count and give thanks for your blessings every day."

— A note to John Wooden from
his father, Joshua Wooden

"You never had to tell any member of the Celtics to dive for a loose ball or to play all-out. We do those things without being reminded."

— John Havlicek

"Don't think that you can make up for it by working twice as hard tomorrow. If you have it within your power to work twice as hard, why aren't you doing it now?"

— John Wooden

"The most important measure of how good a game I had played was how much better I had made my teammates play."

— Bill Russell

"Once practice starts, we work hard, and that's the best conditioning there is. Everything counts. Every little thing counts. Run hard, play hard, go after the ball hard, guard hard. If you play soft (what I call signing a 'non- aggression pact' with your teammates), you won't ever get into shape."

— Pete Carill

"Your reputation will not win games. You must be ready mentally and physically."

— Red Auerbach

Les Wothke on his team:

"We are not real fast. In fact we had three loose balls roll dead yesterday in practice."

"Players need to learn how to play without the ball and without the coach."

— Pete Carill

"Playgrounds are the best place to learn to play the game, because if you lose, you sit down."

— Gary Williams

"A player's ability to rebound is inversely proportional to the distance between where he was born and the nearest railroad tracks. The greater distance you live from the poor side of the railroad tracks, the less likely that you will be a good rebounder."

— Pete Carill

Football

"All football came from Stagg."

— Knute Rockne

"Bear Bryant could take his'n and beat your'n, or he could take your'n and beat his'n."

— Bum Phillips

"Football doesn't take me away from my family life. We've always watched film together."

— Fred Akers

"I want the big play. I'm not going to stay up all night trying to figure out how to gain three yards."

— Sid Gilman

"Raymond Berry was such a great pass receiver he could get free on a subway platform and catch a buttered ear of corn."

— Jack Mann

"If you tell a lie, always rehearse it. If it don't sound good to you, it won't sound good to anyone else."

— Satchel Paige

"Work like a dog. Eat like a horse. Think like a fox. And play like a rabbit."

— George Allen

"All that I accomplished is not because of me. It is because of God and my offensive line."

— Walter Payton

"Speed is not your fastest man, but your slowest man. No back can run faster than his interference."

— Jock Sutherland

"Football doesn't build character. It eliminates the weak ones."

— Darrell Royal

"I love to win. Love it. Football is just too hard and too tough if you're not successful. This isn't just recreation, and the sport isn't for everybody. I just don't want to expend all this time and effort and come up short."

— Bo Schembechler

"Football is blocking and tackling. Everything else is mythology."

— Vince Lombardi

"The forward pass is a cowardly, immoral act."

— Jock Sutherland

"You can learn more character on the two-yard line than anywhere else in life."

— Paul Deitzel

"I'd like to play Army a nine-game schedule. Nobody else but Army."

— Senior Navy football player

"Discipline with team togetherness wins football games."

— Johnny Vaught

"You have to be willing to out-condition your opponents."

— Bear Bryant

"To break training is an act of treason."

— John Heisman

"Be a pragmatist. First, find out what works. Then keep doing it."

— Woody Hayes

"The value of all art, whether in pigment or pigskin, lies to some degree in its resemblance to life."

— Bob Zuppke

"Football is nothing more than a series of mistakes, actions and miscalculations. Punt and let your opponent make the mistakes."

— Bob Neyland

"Running is so natural to me. The feeling of the wind hitting me in the face is incredible. I know that if I can keep that feeling inside me, football will always be fun."

— Eric Dickerson

"You can learn a line from a win; you can learn a book from a defeat."

— Paul Brown

"A team should never practice on a field that is not lined. Your players have to become aware of the field's boundaries."

— John Madden

"Tackling is football. Running is track."

> — **Emlen Tunnell,**
> NFL Hall of Fame safety

"It is the one where the player pitches the ball back to the official after scoring a touchdown."

> — **Bear Bryant**
> (on his favorite play)

"We don't want any candy stripes on our uniforms. These are work clothes."

> — **Darrell Royal**

"Class is when they run you out of town, and it looks like you're leading the parade."

> — **Bill Battle**

"When you find your opponents weak spot, hammer it."

> — **John Heisman**

"My advice to defensive players: Take the shortest route to the ball and arrive in a bad mood."

> — **Bowden Wyatt**

"Michigan's success is due to a policy of letting the enemy take the risk of fumbling inside his forty-yard line."

— Fielding Yost

"There is something in good men that really yearns for discipline and the harsh reality of head to head combat."

— Vince Lombardi

"Football in its purest form, remains a physical fight. As in any fight, if you don't want to fight, it's impossible to win."

— Bud Wilkinson

"Hitting is the one thing that wins games. You make mistakes, but if you are hitting, things will eventually go your way."

— John Mackey

"Everyone has some fear. A man who has no fear belongs in a mental institution, or on special teams."

— Walt Michaels

"You're never as good or as bad as they say you are. In the context of eternity, my football achievements mean very little. To a large extent, my job consists of running downfield, beating a guy and catching a ball – no big deal"

— Steve Largent

Baseball

"What I would like best in the world would be to be 25 again. Putting on those Yankee pinstripes and running out on the field to play ball. I'd give up all my trophies and records just to be able to compete again. The one thing that I both loved and now miss the most is the competition."

— Joe Dimaggio

"Give a boy a bat and a ball and place to play and you'll have a good citizen."

— Joe McCarthy

"The fans like to see home runs, and we have assembled a pitching staff for their enjoyment."

— Clark Griffin,
Minnesota Twins exec

Robin Roberts – on his greatest thrill in an all-star game: " When Mickey Mantle bunted with the wind blowing out in Crosley Field."

"God gets you to the plate, but once you're there, you're on your own."

— Ted Williams

"Hitting is timing. Pitching is upsetting timing."

— Warren Spahn

"You don't save a pitcher for tomorrow. Tomorrow it may rain."

— Leo Durocher

"During my 18 years I came to bat about 10,000 times. I struck out about 1,700 times and walked maybe 1,800 times. If you figure a player will average about 500 at bats a season, that means I played seven years in the major leagues without hitting the ball."

— Mickey Mantle

"All I ever wanted to do in life was play baseball – forever."

— Willie Mays

"One thing you learn as a Cubs fan: When you buy a ticket, you could bank on seeing the bottom of the ninth."

— Joe Garagiola

"A baseball coach once told me that success in life boils down to four simple rules: 'Be on time, wear your uniform, don't throw rocks and stand up in the outfield.'"

— Bob Elliott

"Some days you tame the tiger. Some days the tiger has you for lunch."

— Tug McGraw

"They should move first base back a step to eliminate all those close plays."

— John Lowenstein
Oriole outfielder

"Ninety feet between bases is the nearest to perfection that man has yet achieved."

— Red Smith

"The only statistics I pay close attention to are the number of runs scored and the number of RBI's, because those are the production categories. They are the only ones that help the team win ball games."

— Keith Hernandez

"The charm of baseball is that, dull as it may be on the field, it is endlessly fascinating as a rehash."

— Jim Murray

"Baseball players are the weirdest of all. I think it is all that organ music."

— Peter Gent

"In baseball you are supposed to sit on your butt, spit tobacco and nod at stupid things."

— Bill Lee

"I had to be first all the time – first in everything. All I ever thought about was winning."

— Ty Cobb

"They say I'm the only catcher they had ever seen whose looks improved when he put on the mask."

— Yogi Berra

"In center field you've got too much time to think about everything but baseball."

— Joe Pepitone

"George Brett could get good wood on an aspirin."

— Jim Frey

Ty Cobb, in 1960, explaining why he would hit only .300 against modern-day pitching: "You've got to remember, I'm 73."

"Knowing all about baseball is about as profitable as bein' a good whittler."

— Kin Hubbard

Arthur Baer on Lefty Grove:
"He could throw a lamb chop past a wolf."

"There are three things you can do in a baseball game. You can win, you can lose, or it can rain."

— Casey Stengel

"No matter how good you are you are going to lose one-third of your games. No matter how bad you are you are going to win one-third of your games. It is what you do with other third that makes the difference."

— Tommy Lasorda

"Nobody ever says 'work ball.' They always say 'play ball.' To me that means having fun."

— Willie Stargell

"Go up there and hit what you see. And if you don't see it, come on back."

— Bucky Harris

Golf

"Playing golf you learn a form of meditation. For the four hours you are on the course, you learn to focus on the game and clean your mind of worrisome thoughts. Golf has probably kept more people sane than psychiatrists have."

— Harvey Penick

"Golf is the hardest game in the world to play and the easiest to cheat at."

— Dave Hill

"In golf, when we hit a foul ball, we have to go out and play it."

— Sam Snead

"The best part of golf is that if you observe the etiquette, you can always find a game. I don't care how good you play, you can always find someone who can beat you, and I don't care how bad you play, you can find somebody you can beat."

— Harvey Penick

"Always throw clubs ahead of you. That way, you don't have to waste energy going back to pick them up."

— Tommy Bolt

"Golf is a good walk spoiled."

— Mark Twain

"Golf: A game in which you claim the privileges of age, and retain the playthings of childhood."

— Samuel Johnson

"Golf is a game in which one endeavors to control a ball with implements ill adapted for the purpose."

— Woodrow Wilson

"Golf is a day spent in a round of strenuous idleness."

— **William Wordsworth**

"Golf is a bloodless sport – if you don't count the ulcers."

— **Dick Schaap**
Massacre at Wing Foot

"My favorite shots are the practice swing and the conceded putt."

— **Lord Robertson**

"It is almost impossible to remember how tragic a place the world is when one is playing golf."

— **Robert Lynd**

"Nothing goes down slower than a golf handicap."

— **Bobby Nichols**

"Give me a man with big hands and big feet and no brains, and I'll make a golfer out of him."

— **Walter Hagen**

"Real golfers go to work to relax."

— **George Dillon**

"There are three ways of learning golf: by study, which is the most wearisome; by imitation, which is the most fallacious; and by experience, which is the most bitter."

— Robert Browning

"In almost all other games, you pit yourself against a mortal foe; in golf, it is yourself against the world."

— Arnold Haultain

"I guess there is nothing that will get you mind off everything like golf. I have never been depressed enough to take up the game, but they say you get so sore at yourself you forget to hate your enemies"

— Will Rogers

Sam Snead to a golf pupil: "You've got just one problem. You stand too close to the ball – after you hit it."

"Golf is in the interest of good health and good manners. It promotes self-restraint and affords a chance to play the man and act the gentleman."

— William Taft

"If I had to chose between my wife and my putter, well, I'd miss her."

— Gary Player

"I have three-putted in over forty countries."

— Fred Corcoran

"It is a law of nature that everybody plays a hole badly when going through."

— Bernard Darwin

Inscription on Joe Kirkwood's tombstone:
"Tell your story of hard luck shots, of each shot straight and true; but when you are done, remember son; nobody cares but you."

"Mulligan is a term invented by an Irishman who wanted to hit one more twenty-yard grounder."

— Unknown

"Gimme: an agreement between two golfers who can't putt."

— Jim Bishop

"I would rather play Hamlet with no rehearsal than golf on television."

— Jack Lemmon

"The biggest liar in the world is the golfer who claims he plays the game merely for the exercise."

— Tommy Bolt

"It is impossible to outplay an opponent you cannot out-think."

— Lawson Little

"Golfers as a rule are an exceptionally honest race of men, but uncertain arithmetic is occasionally encountered on the green."

— Henry E. Howland

"Never bet with anyone you meet on the first tee who has a deep suntan, a one iron in his bag and squinty eyes."

— Dave Marr

"I know I'm getting better at golf because I'm hitting fewer spectators."

— Gerald Ford

"It is the constant and undying hope for improvement that makes golf so exquisitely worth playing."

— Bernard Darwin

Harvey Penick, on why he decided to become a teacher: "The first time I watched Sam Snead hit the ball, at that moment I knew that my future was not as a tour player."

"A tolerable day, a tolerable green, a tolerable opponent, supplies, or ought to supply, all that any reasonably constituted human being should require in the way of entertainment."

— A.J. Balfour

Bobby Jones, on how to shoot low scores: "Develop the ability to turn three shots into two."

"Golf is 20 percent mechanics and technique. The other 80 percent is philosophy, humor, tragedy, romance, melodrama, companionship, cussedness and conversation."

— Grantland Rice

"Your financial cost can best be figured when you realize that if you were to devote the same time and energy to business instead of golf, you would be a millionaire in approximately six weeks."

— Buddy Hackett

"A five-foot putt counts one stroke, the same as a 270-yard drive, but the putt may be much more significant to your score."

— Harvey Penick

"Keep your grip pressure light. Arnold Palmer likes to grip the club tightly, but you are not Arnold Palmer."

— Harvey Penick

"Golf is mostly a game of failures."

— Tommy Aaron

"If you lose your temper, you will most likely lose the match."

— Horace Hutchinson

"If profanity had any influence on the flight of the ball, the game would be played far better than it is."

— **Horace Hutchinson**

"Golf combines two favorite American pastimes: taking long walks, and hitting things with a stick."

— **P.J. O'Rourke,**
Modern Manners

"The worst club in my bag is my brain."

— **Chris Perry**

"I played with a guy that took twenty-one waggles before he could swing the club. People in his foursome would look the other way when it was his turn to hit."

— **Harvey Penick**

"Easy, I missed a 20-footer for a 12."

— **Arnold Palmer**
(on how he made a 13 on a hole)

"I don't care to join any club that is prepared to have me as a member."

— **Groucho Marx**

"The hardest shot is a mashie at 90 yards from the green, where the ball has to be played against an oak tree, bounced back into a sand trap, hits a stone, bounces on the green, and then rolls into the cup. That shot is so difficult, I have only made it once."

— Zeppo Marx

"If you watch a game, it's fun. If you play it, it's recreation. If you work at it, it's golf."

— Bob Hope

"It took me 17 years to get 3000 hits in baseball. I did it in one afternoon on the golf course."

— Hank Aaron

"Baseball players quit playing, and they take up golf. Basketball players quit, take up golf. Football players quit and take up golf. What are we supposed to take up when we quit?"

— George Archer

"Golf is an ideal diversion, but a ruinous disease."

— Bertie Charles Forbes

"I owe everything to golf. Where else could a guy with an IQ like mine make this much money?"

— Hubert Green

"My sole ambition in the game is to do well enough to give it up."

— David Feherty

Football player Lawrence Taylor, on being late for practice:
"It wasn't my fault, blame the guys in the foursome in front of us."

Harvey Penick on Ben Crenshaw:
"Ben came to me when he was about eight years old. We cut off a seven iron for him. I showed him a good grip, and we went outside. There was a green about seventy-five yards away. I asked Ben to tee up a ball and hit it onto the green. He did. Then I said 'Now let's go to the green and putt the ball into the hole.'
'If you wanted it in the hole, why didn't you tell me the first time?'"

"If a lot of people gripped a knife and fork like they do a golf club, they'd starve to death."

— Sam Snead

"No sir. We couldn't have coincidence like that."

— Scottish caddie
(on being told he was the worst caddie in the world)

"The person I fear most in the last two rounds is myself."

— Tom Watson

"I'd give up golf if I didn't have so many sweaters."

— **Bob Hope**

"I was three over – one over the house, one over the patio, and one over the swimming pool."

— **George Brett**

"Give me golf clubs, fresh air and a beautiful partner, and you can keep my golf clubs and the fresh air."

— **Jack Benny**

"It will take three fine shots to get there in two sir."

— **Scottish caddie**

"Golf is the only game in the world in which a precise knowledge of the rules can earn one a reputation for bad sportsmanship."

— **Patrick Campbell**
How to Become a Scratch Golfer

"Action before thought is the ruination of most of your shots."

— **Tommy Armour**
How to Play Your Best Golf All the Time

"The game can be played in company or alone. Robinson Crusoe on his island, with his man Friday as a caddie, could have realized the golfer's dream of perfect happiness – a fine day, a good course and a clear green."

— Henry E. Rowland

"The higher your score, the faster you can lower it—with the short game."

— Harvey Penick

"He is the boldest of all the players. The game has never seen one like him. The epitaph on his tombstone ought to read: 'Here lies Arnold Palmer. He went for the green.'"

— Mark McCormack
Arnie: The Evolution of a Legend

"It is not how good your good shots are, it is how bad are your bad ones."

— Unknown

Craig Stadler's reply, when asked why he was using a new putter: "The old one didn't float too well."

"If you pick up a golfer and hold it close to your ear, like a conch shell, and listen, you will hear an alibi."

— Fred Beck

"The cup is only one inch wide for a putt that is struck too hard. The cup is four inches wide for a ball that dies in the hole."

— Harvey Penick

"There is one essential only in the golf swing: The ball must be hit."

— Sir Walter Simpson

"Those who cannot drive suppose themselves to be good putters."

— Sir Walter Simpson

"The majority treat the hole as place more difficult to get into than it really is."

— Sir Walter Simpson

"Golf has drawbacks. It is possible, by too much of it, to destroy your mind."

— Sir Walter Simpson

"A secret disbelief in the enemy's play is very useful for match play."

— Sir Walter Simpson

"Through all the years of experience, I have found that air offers less resistance than dirt."

— Jack Nicklaus

"The difference between golf and government is that in golf you can't improve your lie."

— George Deukmejian

"A round of golf requires no more than 3 hours and 15 minutes. If you are on the course longer than this, a marshal will come escort you off."

— Sign on a Scottish golf course

"I never wanted to be a millionaire. I just wanted to live like one."

— Walter Hagen

"A high handicapper will be surprised at how often the mind will make the muscles hit the ball to the target, even with a far less than perfect swing."

— Harvey Penick

"Harbour Town is so tough, even your clubs get tired."

— Charles Price

"It's Star Wars golf. The place was designed by Darth Vader."

—Ben Crenshaw
(on the Tournament Players Club
at Sawgrass, Bury Me In
a Pot Bunker)

"It matters not the sacrifice which makes the duffer's wife so sore. I am the captive of my slice. I am the servant of my score."

— Grantland Rice

"Never have so many spent so much to sit in relative comfort to brag about their failures."

— Keith Jackson

"You can talk to a fade, but a hook won't listen."

— Lee Trevino

"He told me to keep the ball low."

— Chi Chi Rodriguez
(advice his caddie gave him
on a putt)

"Don't be afraid of a player with a good grip and a bad swing. Don't be afraid of a player with a bad grip and a good swing. The player to beware of is the one with the bad grip and the bad swing. If he has reached your level, he has grooved his faults and knows how to score."

— Harvey Penick

Jimmy Demaret on Bob Hope's golfing ability:
"Bob has beautiful short game. Unfortunately, off the tee."

"The least little thing upsets him on the links. He missed a short putt because of the uproar of butterflies in the adjoining meadows."

— P. G. Wodehouse

"I don't say my golf game is bad, but if I grew tomatoes they'd come up sliced."

— Miller Barber

"You would like to gather up several holes from Prestwick and mail them to you top ten enemies."

— Dan Jenkins

"Don't tell me you are too old and your nerves so frayed that you can't putt. Every golf course has a few old geezers who can chip and putt the eyes out of the cup."

— Harvey Penick

"A good golf course is like good music or good anything else. It is not necessarily a course which appeals the first time one plays it, but one which grows on the player the more frequently they visit it."

— Alister MacKenzie

Miscellaneous

"On game day I am more nervous than a pig in a packing plant."

— Darrell Royal

"Let us be thankful for the fools. But not for them, the rest of us could not succeed."

— Mark Twain

"I'll eat anything that won't eat me."

— Herman Hickman

"I give the same halftime speech over and over. It works best when my players are better than the other teams players."

— Chuck Mills

Running back George Rogers when asked about the upcoming season: "I want to rush for 1,000 or 1.500 yards, whichever comes first."

"I fought Sugar Ray so many times, it is a wonder that I didn't get diabetes."

— Jake LaMotta

"I demand just one thing from my players, that is attitude. I want them to think as positively as an 85-year old man who married a 25-year old woman and bought a five-bedroom house near an elementary school."

— Charlie Pell

"When you are a coach, you are miserable. When you are not a coach, you're more miserable."

— Fred Shero

Football commentator and former player Joe Theisman: "Nobody in football should be called a genius. A genius is a guy like Norman Einstein."

Wilber Evans talking about baseball coach Bibb Falk:
"Bibb is so dedicated to baseball that until a week or so ago, he thought the first verse in the Bible said, 'In the big inning, God created heaven and earth."

"Prayer never seems to work for me on the golf course. I think it has something to do with my being a terrible putter."

— Rev. Billy Graham

"Wherever fast players go, they get there faster than slow players."

— Pete Carill

"If three people say you are an ass, put on a bridle."

— Spanish proverb

"We wouldn't worry nearly as much about what others thought of us…. If we recognized how seldom they did."

— Unknown

"You guys line up alphabetically by height," and "you guys pair up in groups of three, then line up in a circle."

— Bill Peterson –
Florida State football coach

"I had one real good kid in Florida to recruit. I really worked on the parents, believing that to be the best method. Coach Bear Bryant of Alabama worked on the boy. I dined and danced the boys' mother. The boy went to Alabama, the mother enrolled at Miami."

— Otis Mooney,
Miami football coach

After a very tough series of losses, Lou Holtz opened his TV show with these words: "Welcome to the Lou Holtz Show. Unfortunately, I am Lou Holtz."

"I'd run over my mother to win the Super Bowl."

— Russ Grimm

"I'd run over Grimm's mother too."

— Matt Millen

"The sun doesn't shine on the same dog's butt everyday, but we sure as heck didn't expect a near total eclipse."

— Steve Sloan

Don Zimmer – on why he arrives several hours early for a game: "I want to make sure nobody's in my uniform."

"I'm going to graduate on time, no matter how long it takes."

— Senior basketball player –
University of Pittsburgh

"We are not allowed to comment on the lousy officiating."

— Jim Finks–
New Orleans Saints
(after a loss)

Don Manoukian, Oakland Raiders guard when asked how he wanted his steak cooked: "Just knock the breath out of it."

Freshman football player at Clemson who was ineligible because of academic requirements: "I play football. I'm not trying to be a professor. The tests don't seem to make sense to me, measuring your brain on stuff I haven't been through in school."

"We were so poor, every time my Mom tossed the dog a bone, he had to signal for a fair catch, else all the kids would beat him to it."

— David "Smokey" Gaines

"They are always talking about eliminating the big man by raising the basket. If they want to change the game, have 'em bore a hole in the floor and change the rules so you have to drop the ball through the hole. Then there would be cheatin' to sign up little men. Everybody would be chasin' after guys two-feet tall."

— Abe Lemons

Boxing promoter Dan Duva on Mike Tyson hooking up again with promoter Don King: "Why would anyone expect him to come out smarter? He went to prison for three years, not Princeton."

"We don't care how big or strong our opponents are, as long as they are human."

— Bob Zuppke

"Trust everybody in the game, but always cut the cards."

— Anonymous

"Never ask a barber if he thinks you need a haircut."

— Unknown

Dizzy Dean – as he pulled into a gas station:
"It puzzles me how they know what corners are good for filling stations. Just how did these fellows know there was gas and oil under here?"

"They say that the breaks even up in the long run. But who has the endurance or the contract to last that long?"

— **Bum Phillips**
Houston Oilers

Yogi Berra when asked one spring what his cap size was:
    "How do I know? I'm not in shape yet."

"If you are sure you understand everything that is going on, you are hopelessly confused."

— **Anonymous**

"Some of us are like wheelbarrows – only useful when pushed and very easily upset."

— **Jack Hebert**

Stu Grimson, Chicago Blackhawks, explaining why he keeps a color photo of himself above his locker:

"That is so when I forget how to spell my name, I can still find my clothes."

"Who needs five guys running around out on the court with your paycheck?"

— **Johnny Kerr**

"I started out with nothing… I still have most of it."

— **Unknown**

"Winning coaches always remember that there is only a one-foot difference between a halo and a noose."

— **Bobby Bowden,**
Florida State football

Lou Duva, veteran boxing trainer, on heavyweight Andrew Golata: "He gets up at six o'clock in the morning regardless of what time it is."

Abe Lemons on curfews: "Oh, I have one, I guess. It's 2 am on July 4th. They all have to be in by then. If going to bed at 10 o'clock makes you play good, why don't we have 'em go to bed in the afternoon about 3?"

Chuck Nevitt, North Carolina State basketball player, explaining to Coach Jim Valvano why he appeared so nervous at practice: "My sister is expecting a baby, and I don't know if I'm going to be an aunt or an uncle."

Abe Lemons on roles: "At the University of Texas, if they need a yard, they give the ball to Earl Campbell. They don't give it to some clown because he is a nice guy."

"Egotism is the anesthetic that dulls the pain of stupidity."

— Frank Leahy

"We can't win at home. We can't win on the road. I just can't figure out where else to play."

— Pat Williams –
Orlando Magic GM

Bill Lee – when asked how much pressure he was feeling late in a game: "Thirty-two pounds per square inch at sea level."

"Remember, even a kick in the butt, results in a step forward."

— Unknown

"You don't know a ladder has splinters until you slide down it."

— Bum Phillips

"You draw the Xs and Os on a blackboard. That isn't so difficult, I can do it with my left hand."

— John McKay

Alan Kulwicki, stock car driver, on racing on Saturday nights as opposed to Sunday afternoons: "It's basically the same, just darker."

"Relax. You only have so many heartbeats. If you use 'em too quick, you go too fast."

— Abe Lemons

" Money can't buy happiness, but it can buy you the kind of misery you prefer."

— Anonymous

"If they ever drop a nuclear bomb on this country, the only things that will survive are astroturf and Don Shula."

— Bubba Smith

Abe Lemons when asked by a player why he wasn't playing more: "I don't like you, I don't like your mother, don't like your dad, don't like your dog, don't like anything about you." It satisfied him.

"Never get into an argument about cesspools with an expert."

— Grandmother's advice to Grantland Rice

"One day of good practice is like one day of clean livin', it ain't gonna help."

— Abe Lemons

"You can observe a lot just by watching."

— Yogi Berra

"If there is any larceny in a man, golf will bring it out."

— Paul Gallico

"I told my players that if they won, I would give them jewels, cars, girls, anything they wanted. When they won, they wanted to know where their stuff was. I told them I checked during the game and learned it was against NCAA rules."

— Abe Lemons

"They say a tie is like kissing your sister. I guess that is better than kissing your brother."

— Lou Holtz

Lou Holtz – On over exuberant fans pelting him with oranges while celebrating Arkansas's invitation to the Orange Bowl: "I'm glad we weren't invited to the Gator Bowl."

"Some coaches pray for wisdom. I pray for 260-pound tackles. They will give me plenty of wisdom."

— Chuck Mills

"If people don't want to come out to the park, nobody's going to stop them."

— Yogi Berra

"A closed mouth gathers no feet."

— Unknown

"Dick Butkus was like Moby Dick in a goldfish bowl."

— Steve Sabol

Frank Layden, Utah Jazz president, on a former player: "I asked him, 'Son what is it with you? Is it ignorance or apathy?' He said, 'Coach, I don't know and I don't care.'"

Abe Lemons – on press brochures:
"Just once I'd like to see a picture of one of these guys with the caption — 'He's a dog' underneath it. 'Ate up $8,000 worth of groceries in four years and can't play worth a lick'."

Pete Gent – describing Tom Landry's enormous playbook to a rookie: "Don't bother reading it kid. Everybody gets killed in the end.

"Indecision is the key to flexibility."
— Brad Homes

"All those football coaches who hold dressing room prayers before a game should be forced to attend church once a week."
— Duffy Daugherty

"If the meek are going to inherit the earth, our offensive linemen are going to be land barons."
— Bill Muir
SMU football coach

"You can't tell anything from spring practice. It's like having your daughter come in at four in the morning with a Gideon Bible."
— Dan Fambrough

"You can say something to popes, kings and presidents, but you can't talk to an official. In the next war, they ought to give everybody a whistle."

— Abe Lemons

"May those who love us, love us, And those who don't love us, may god turn their hearts. And if he can't turn their hearts, may he turn their ankles, so we will know them by their limping."

— An old Gaelic blessing

"An expert is someone who knows more and more about less and less."

— Anonymous

"When I caught the ball, it was a bright sunny day. By the time I got in the end zone, it was partly cloudy."

— George Martin
NY Giants defensive end

"Always remember that Goliath was a 40-point favorite over David."

— Shug Jordan

"Before our last game, an anonymous fan left a fruitcake for the coaches. I wouldn't let them eat it. When you are 2 and 8, you don't mess around with unsigned fruitcakes."

— Lee Corso

"Lombardi has to have the highest threshold of pain in the world – none of our injuries hurts him at all."

— **Jerry Kramer**
Green Bay Packers

"The problem here at Yale is to win enough to keep the alumni sullen and not mutinous."

— **Herman Hickman**

"If hockey fights were fake, you would see me in more of them."

— **Rod Gilbert**
New York Rangers

"The only way to stop Jim Brown was to get him a movie contract."

— **Spider Lockhart**

"Just give every coach the same amount of money and tell them they can keep what's left over."

—**Abe Lemons' solution to recruiting excesses**

"Yesterday is a canceled check. Today is cash on the line. Tomorrow is a promissory note."

— **Hank Stram**

"It was so bad that the players were giving each other high fives when they hit the rim."

> — **John Shumate**
> S.E. Missouri State basketball coach
> (on his weak team)

"I wouldn't say Earl Campbell was in a class by himself, but I can tell you one thing: it sure don't take long to take roll."

> — **Bum Phillips**

Abe Lemons – on team rules:

"If I make a set of rules, then some guy goes out and steals an airplane. He comes back and says 'it wasn't on the list of rules'."

"I tackle everybody and throw them away one at a time until I come to the one who has the ball."

> — **Big Daddy Lipscomb**

"He who falls in love with himself will have no rivals."

> — **Anonymous**

"Walter Payton is the best back in football. I wish I had better words to describe him."

> — **Bud Grant**

"Good things come to those who waiteth, if he worketh like heck while he waiteth."

> — **Bill Foster**

"On this team, we are all united in a common goal: to keep my job."

— Lou Holtz

"I could have been a Rhodes Scholar, except for my grades."

— Duffy Daugherty

"Depend on the rabbits foot for luck, if you will, but remember it didn't work for the rabbit."

— R. E. Shay

"He who is late, may knaw the bones."

— Yugoslav proverb

"We will never offer a scholarship for rowing. Clemson will not subsidize a sport where a man sits on his butt and goes backward."

— Frank Howard

"Franco Harris faked me out so bad that I got a 15 yard penalty for grabbing my own face mask."

— D.D. Lewis

"I never graduated from college, but I was there two terms: Truman's and Eisenhower's."

— Alex Karras

About the Author

Bruce Eamon Brown is a special presenter for the NAIA's "Champions of Character Program." Previously, he served as the athletic director at Northwest College in Kirkland, Washington. A retired coach, he worked at every level of education in his more than three decades of teaching and coaching. His coaching experiences included basketball, football, volleyball, and baseball at the junior high and high school levels, and basketball at the junior college and college levels. He was involved with championship teams at each level of competition.

Brown is a much sought-after speaker, who frequently addresses coaches, players, and parents on selected aspects concerning participation in sport. He has written several books, including the highly acclaimed *Another 1001 Motivational Messages and Quotes: Featuring the 7 Essentials of Great Teams*. He has also been the featured speaker on several well-received instructional videos:

- *Basketball Skills and Drills for Younger Players: Volume 7 – Individual Defense*
- *Basketball Skills and Drills for Younger Players: Volume 8 – Team Defense*
- *Basketball Skills and Drills for Younger Players: Volume 9 – Fast Break*
- *Basketball Skills and Drills for Younger Players: Volume 10 – Zone Offense*
- *Basketball Skills and Drills for Younger Players: Volume 11 – The Role of Parents in Athletics*
- *Fun Ways to End Basketball Practice*
- *Team Building Through Positive Conditioning*
- *Redefining the Term "Athlete" – Using the Five Core Values*
- *How to Teach Character Through Sport*

Brown and his wife, Dana, have five daughters, Allison, Katie, Shannon, Bridget, and Dana. The family resides in Camano Island, Washington.

Additional Resources from Bruce Brown and Coaches Choice

Books:

- **Teaching Character Through Sport**
  2003 • 140 pages • 1-58518-729-1 • $19.95

- **Another 1001 Motivational Messages and Quotes**
  2003 • 160 pages • 1-58518-847-6 • $19.95

Videos:

- **How To Teach Character Through Sport**
  2003 • 58 minutes • 827008734832 • $40.00

- **Redefining the Term "Athlete" – Using the Five Core Values**
  2003 • 31 minutes • 827008733033 • $40.00

- **The Role of Parents in Athletics**
  2002 • 46 minutes • 827008641437 • $40.00

- **Team Building Through Positive Conditioning**
  2002 • 62 minutes • 827008661930 • $40.00

To Place Your Order:

Toll Free: 888-229-5745
Mail: Coaches Choice
P.O. Box 1828
Monterey, CA 93942
FAX: 831-372-6075
ONLINE: www.coacheschoice.com